As you Go, Along the Way!
A Journey of Discovery and Journaling with God

An inspirational book of short stories, devotionals, poems, encouraging words and journaling to help you deepen and further your journey with God the Father, His son Jesus Christ and The Holy Spirit.

Madeline Y. Brownfield

Copyright © 2021 Madeline Y. Brownfield

As You Go, Along The Way - A Journey of Discovery and Journaling with God

All rights reserved. No part of this publication may be reproduced, distributed, or transmitted in any form or by any means, including photocopying, recording, or other electronic or mechanical methods, without the prior written permission of the publisher, except in the case of brief quotations embodied in critical reviews and certain other noncommercial uses permitted by copyright law. For permission requests, write to the publisher, addressed "Attention: Permissions Coordinator," at the address below.

TDS Publishing
P.O. Box 161
Lithia Springs, GA 30122
www.terrydswain.com

Published in association with Lulu Press, Inc, Morrisville, NC.

All Scripture quotations, unless otherwise indicated, are taken from the Holy Bible: King James Version®, KJV®. Copyright © 1973, 1978, 1984, 2011 by International Bible Society. Used by permission of TDS Publishing. All rights reserved.

Scripture quotations marked NIV are taken from the Holy Bible, New International Version.

ISBN 978-1-716-65447-3

Cover photograph by Brandon C. Brownfield
Cover designed by Daniel Harris, Danmanz Designs

Printed in the United States of America

Contents

Acknowledgements	
Dedication	
The Adoption	page 7
As You Go, Along The Way	page 11
Broken, Yet Beautifully	page 15
The Prodigal	page 21
Love Song	page 31
Hope	page 37
And God Said	page 41
Heavenly Perspective	page 47
At The End Of It All	page 53
The Spirit of the Fear of the Lord	page 59
Surely Goodness and Mercy	page 69
The Book of Amos	page 81
Who Does Christ Say I Am	page 85
Love Is	page 91
Thou Prepares a Table	page 96
Prayer	page 102
Wisdom And Understanding	page 109
Endurance	page 114
He That Dwells	page 123
Strong	page 127
Purge Me With Hyssop	page 133
The Simplicity of the Gospel	page 139
Why	page 143

Acknowledgments

I would like to give special thanks to the following who helped me to bring this journey to realization.

First and foremost is my Lord and Savior Jesus Christ who without Him this could have never happened. It was and still is my love for Him that began so many years ago where I began writing **"Dear God"** letters expressing to Him all of my hopes, dreams, and desires.

Secondly, my husband, Russell B. Brownfield, Jr., who without his love, patience and personal cheerleading, I would have not had the courage to step out and bring this work to completion.

Thirdly, I'd like to thank my children Brandon Brownfield, Breana Brownfield, and my daughter in love O'Livia Brownfield. Their great input helped me to make this work even better than I could have possibly imagined.

I would also like to thank Prophet Greg Beacham, the man whom the Lord used to give me one of my first words of prophecy. Through this man, the Lord told me to continue journaling and writing and that with my voice God would bring many into the Kingdom. I had no idea what prophecy was at that time, but that moment changed my life because this man whom I'd just met, should have had no idea except by the Holy Spirit that I had been writing my prayers and journaling since the age of eleven. I recognized God speaking to me personally at that moment and the heavenly encouragement and exhortation was happily received with meditation and prayer. And last, but certainly not least, I would like to thank my New Water International Ministries family of Davenport, Iowa. That prophetic ministry under the leadership of Apostles Tawunya and Leonard Hicks, taught me to hear the voice of the Lord prophetically and to speak what I'd hear or see, either by prophesying or intercessory prayer, dreams and visions. Although I didn't know it at first, this was my training ground and I am forever grateful to them and the prophets in that ministry who took the time and patience to pray with me and for me, train me, listen to me, speak life into me and allow me the privilege to follow them across the country while serving with them and others. All of these opportunities played a significant role in cutting my teeth in prophetic ministry.

Family, I pray this book makes you proud and all those who've helped me along the way, even in the smallest of ways, may it bring you joy and enrich your journey with the Father in some way. I love you all!

Dedication

I would like to dedicate this book to all those who need a little encouragement.

To those who have lost their way in this life and lost sight of what is truly important - their relationship with Jesus Christ.

To those who have been distracted, hurt, depressed, oppressed, down-trodden, and can't seem to find the good in everyday.

This book-devotional-journal is dedicated to you all to help reawaken what God has put within you: the creativity, genius, uniqueness, purpose and spark of life. This book-devotional-journal was created to help you strengthen your walk with Jesus Christ and to help you find your way back to the Lord and the love He has for you. He wants you to know that you are LOVED with an unfailing, perfected love from Father God. And my hope also is that you will use the gifts He has deposited within each of you to bring Him glory.

So, as you read this book it may serve as a devotional and/or journal; if you feel inspired to pray, write, draw, sing, imagine, create, prophesy, teach, preach or whatever the Lord puts upon your heart, go ahead and do it. Remember, He put it there for you to offer it back to Him in praise and worship and through the daily living of your life: GIVE HIM THE GLORY!

My prayer Father is that you would bless these pages to be an encouragement to the reader. Bless the person reading this book and journaling in these pages to the point that their gifts will be stirred and begin to flow like rivers of living waters just as your Word says, for Your glory God. I pray that Your Holy Spirit will ignite and set ablaze their hearts to find and/or renew their LOVE, passion and zeal for you Lord. In Jesus name I pray Amen.

THE ADOPTION

"HAVING PREDESTINATED US UNTO THE ADOPTION OF CHILDREN BY JESUS CHRIST TO HIMSELF, ACCORDING TO THE GOOD PLEASURE OF HIS WILL."

I was alone and lost. I came upon the steps of a warmly lit inviting place. The glow of golden warm lights shown through the windows from the street and the smell of food wafted in the air. I inhaled deeply the lovely smells as my stomach gave a loud rumble. It had been a full twenty-four hours since my last little meal and I was past hungry.

This place had no sign. I had no idea where I was or how I ended up there. Besides the aroma of the food in the air, there was this silent pull. "Where was I?" I couldn't seem to stop staring at the place, taking in the beautiful smells and the warm glow coming from the windows. Why wouldn't my feet move? I couldn't walk away, yet I couldn't move forward up the stairs to the front door either. What was wrong with me?

Suddenly, I had a flashback to my childhood as a kid who grew up with too much: entitled, and ungrateful. In the last three years I'd began to rebel. I fell into addiction, depression, disappointments, homelessness, rejection, heartbreak and suicide attempts. Now, no longer a kid, yet not quite an adult, I'd go into a rage when things didn't go my way. That was usually when my father wouldn't give me more money because he knew what I'd do with it. So, I would steal it from my mom's purse, then go out on a alcohol or drug binge.

Well, my family had finally had enough. My father cut me off and threw me out of the house. I had no job, no skills, no money and after six months of crashing on friends couches, sleeping in bus terminals and doorways, eating anything I could from the generosity of strangers, I found myself here. Here at the steps of what looks like a misplaced house in the midst of these high rises and businesses. What was I doing here? My stomach snapped me back into the here and now and I thought to myself, "Just put one foot in front of the other and go up the stairs." My stomach gave me courage.

When I got to the top of the stairs, I knocked on the door a few times. It took an unusually long time for someone to answer and I almost lost my courage and was about to turn around and go back down the stairs. Then, to my surprise a man answered. I don't know what or who I was expecting, but not Him. He was a man in His early thirties I guessed who greeted me with a big smile and compassionate eyes. He said, "Come in" all friendly like, as if He knew me. I smiled a nervous smile at him, as I crossed the threshold of the door now behind me. I instantly felt the warmth and peace of the place, as I looked around from where I stood. It was amazing. I had never in my life felt such a warmth and sense of peace that seemed to touch every fiber of my being. I almost melted to the floor. It was overwhelming. He asked me if I was hungry. I immediately nodded my head nervously, Yes! As I followed Him to the kitchen I began to notice the others: other children of all ages, colors, sizes and nationalities.

They quietly played games, talked amongst themselves, smiled and giggled with each other. Again, suddenly, I felt something inside of me that I can honestly say I had never felt before, but I didn't quite understand what it was. It felt good! My whole being became alive as I became more and more aware of it. But what was it? We finally arrived at this huge bright kitchen with a large, lengthy table. A pot of something good simmered on the stove. The man with the big smile and compassionate eyes said, "Have a seat and make yourself at home." He sat a glass of milk in front of me, then He went to the stove and ladled me out a bowl of warm stew and cut me a nice slice of bread. Man! My eyes got big and my mouth watered in anticipation of what I knew was gonna be goooooood! I dug in.

The man with the big smile smiled even bigger as He watched me eat that delicious bowl of stew. It seemed to give Him joy, and I was happy to oblige. He soon left me to enjoy my meal as He attended to the other things in the kitchen. After the meal, we went into the family room where most of the other children were quietly playing. We sat down. Each in a comfy chair facing each other next to the fireplace. I could immediately feel the warmth of the fire. It completely warmed over every part of me that the wonderful stew had already begun to warm. As I began to settle

in my chair, He asked me about myself. I hesitated for a moment thinking "What a mess!"

Then I began to tell Him my story; how I had what seemed to from all appearances to be the ideal life. I had everything my parents could afford: anything I wanted. But that soon turned into me being spoiled with feelings of entitlement, which turned into disobedience, rebellion, drugs, depression and suicide attempts. That was the beginning of a vicious cycle. I would do better for a while only to fall right back into the drugs, alcohol, depression, and suicide attempts; and eventually intervention.

As I talked, I noticed His smile faded just a bit and His eyes filled even more compassion; if that were at all possible. I got lost in His eyes. I felt His compassion and LOVE. Yes! Voile! That was it! The LOVE He had for me and all of the children in this home. It was Genuine LOVE. An unusual feeling, but now not so new since being in this house and in His presence.

You see, although my parents loved me the best way they knew how, with things, money and privilege, I'd never experienced a real and deep love like I was experiencing right now. Love that seemed to radiate out of Him. I honestly didn't know how to process these new feelings that seemed to envelope me like a big, soft, cuddly blanket from the inside out. I noticed that I'd stopped talking and I was just starring at Him. I started to weep. I didn't understand what had suddenly come over me. Deep repentant sobs flowed out from a deep deep part of me that I wasn't familiar with. I couldn't control it and I didn't want to: I needed this! This felt cleansing. This felt good.

The other children had stopped playing and they all gathered around me with soft smiles on their faces as if they knew what was taking place. They must have seen this before; many times. The gentle man with the big smile and compassionate eyes said, "My father who is rich in houses and land has room for you here if you would like stay. This is a special place where we welcome in the lost, the rejected, the broken hearted, and the abandoned. Those who have lost hope. Having predestined this very moment; your adoption unto Himself through Me. My name is Jesus and I would love for you to accept my invitation to come and stay."

Just then, He extended his hand out to me waiting for me to take it and accept His invitation. I said to Him, "Me!

After everything I just told you, you still want me?" "Yes" He said. "There is nothing you have done in your past, nor nothing that you could ever do in your future, that could ever take away the Love that I and my Father have for you away." Still looking into His eyes, I noticed He had a tear. He seemed to feel all of my pain and disappointments and rejection. He seemed to understand, and so I took His hand and said "Yes!" And everything but Him seemed to fade away. At that moment, it was just Him and me. My pain faded. My sorrow faded. My mistakes and bad decisions faded. I felt different. I felt new. I knew in that moment that I was loved and wanted.

The other children let out a roar of cheering, applause and celebration that filled the entire house. I told Jesus "Yes" and now I belong to Him and the Father. I am accepted. I am wanted. I am ADOPTED. I am SAVED. I am one among the brethren of Jesus Christ; the gentle man with the big smile and compassionate eyes: MY SAVIOR, MY REDEEMER, MY LORD!

AS YOU GO, ALONG THE WAY!

This the Lord gave me a couple of years ago with a word he had me share with a mother in our church. She wanted and needed prayer for healing in a knee that had undergone a surgical replacement. The knee was still giving her pain, and swelling. While praying, the Lord suddenly impressed upon me that her knee would be healed as she believed and continued in faith, walking her healing out.

Matthew 8:13, "And Jesus said unto the centurion, **Go thy way**; and as thou has believed, so be it done unto thee. And his servant was healed in the selfsame hour.

Luke 17:12-14, "And as he entered into a certain village, there met him ten men that were lepers, which stood afar off: And they lifted up their voices, and said, Jesus, Master, have mercy on us. And when he saw them, he said unto them, Go shew yourselves unto the priests. And it came to pass, that **as they went**, they were cleansed."

AS WE GO!

Because the Lord doesn't reveal everything to us all at once, the more steps we take in faith, the more He reveals,
the more He releases and
the more treasures within us are opened,
the more gifts of the Spirit are ignited, activated and strengthened.

As we go! Along the way! He gives us more and more and more of His plan for us as we walk this journey out with Him in faith.

Matthew 25:21, "His lord said unto him, Well done, thou good and faithful servant: thou hast been faithful over a few things, I will make thee ruler over many things: enter thou into the joy of thy lord". God will expand our capacity to receive more of Him if we simply ask in faith and steward well what He has already given us.

If you will not despise your small beginnings,
but cherish them,
      steward them diligently,
           show the Lord that you value what He has given you.

Zechariah 4:10, "For who hath despised the day of small things?",
He will increase it and give you more.

      But we have to move.
           We have to trust.
                We have to show God that we believe what He says.

So As You Go in Faith!

The Lord says, Along The Way, you will posses new land and territory. Like running water that moves and flows carving out creeks, rivers and streams, the movement, the momentum, the force of it claims, possesses, and impacts. And You will impact and see the new and exciting things to come. You will see miracles, signs and wonders.

But be ye doers of the word, and not hearers only, deceiving your own selves. James 1:22 KJV

…ye shall be holy, for I the LORD your God am holy. Leviticus 19:2 KJV

Broken, Yet Beautiful

Holy Spirit brought back to my remembrance today while I was reading His word, the vision He gave me: a clay pot pitcher with a crack in it's side. So He elaborated on the vision.

The pitcher was ordinary looking; not beautiful in any way by human standards. From a human perspective, this clay pitcher would be considered 'unusable' and thrown away. But the Lord showed me that day, that I was that clay pitcher formed by the Master's hands. And although His original design for me was perfect, life left me bruised and beaten by this world. Yet, in His eyes I was still precious. He said I was still useful to Him.

He showed me that I am still able to receive from Him and pour out. That imperfection that came by the hurt, disappointments and betrayal, God turned it around so that it still worked out for my good. Genesis 50:20 says, "But as for you, (*Satan*) ye thought evil against me; but God meant it unto good, to bring to pass, as it is this day to save much people alive." Romans 8:28 says, "And we know that all things work together for the good to them that love God, to them who are called according to His purpose.

That weakness in me, is made strong by the blood of Jesus Christ. The love He showed and the blood He shed on Calvary makes me strong. He showed me this as He filled the pitcher with water (*Holy Spirit*), and picked it up and carried it to it's intended place and purpose, the small crack leaked water (*Holy Spirit, anointing, power, authority, healing, prayers, encouragement, comfort, exhortation, care, compassion, service, love*), it leaked, watered, nourished, sustained, fed those it encountered as it was carried along the way.

Remember the story when Jesus was **on His way** to the Jewish ruler's house to heal the ruler's very sick and soon dead 12 year old daughter? **On His way**, as He went, a woman with an issue of blood for 12 years touched the hem of His garment. Virtue left Him and she was healed. When He left the Jewish leaders house, as He went, He healed two blind men **along the way**. And oh, He also raised that young girl from the dead! Hallelujah!

As He went, carried by the Holy Spirit, without the intention to do a miracle in the interim, He heals and opens blinded eyes. **ALONG THE WAY**, as you let yourself be carried by Jesus Christ, it's important to note that you can't be still, you have to move and let yourself be used by Him. Your imperfections will serve a purpose **AS YOU GO**, because of the Holy Ghost inside of you. You may leak, but from your belly will flow rivers of living waters and you will bless others **ALONG THE WAY** as you move toward your healing and being made whole. **So Move! GO!**

Some plant, some water, but it is God who gives the increase and gets the glory. 1 Corinthians 3:6-7

That crack, leak, imperfection put upon you by the world only added to the watering of the soil, added to the growth and nourishment of seeds already sown and growth to the Kingdom of God. He showed me and reassured me that although imperfect right now, He is perfecting all that concerns me and you (Psalm 138:8). And He can, will and IS using me and you for His glory as long as you let Him. He will not force Himself upon you.

I am Broken, yet Beautiful. Remembering His promise. "Being confident of this very thing, that He which hath begun a good work in you will perform it until the day of Jesus Christ." Philippians 1:6

Let yourself be used by God JUST AS YOU ARE: perfect imperfections; broken yet beautiful for His Glory and His Honor. You are still valuable to God and needed for His Kingdom work. You are beautiful to Him.

Even if your vessel is completely broken, YOU ARE BEAUTIFUL, VALUABLE, STILL USEABLE, and MOST DEFINITELY LOVED!

HE SEES YOU! HE KNOWS YOU!
Offer up to Him the broken pieces of your clay pot and watch what He does. If you let Him, He'll work it out to 'save many lives', the likes of which you may not know until seated together in heaven.

Father I pray that the person reading this right now, will surrender to you the broken pieces of their lives. I pray that the person reading this will know that they are loved and wanted by You. I pray that they will let themselves be used by You, imperfections and all because You Lord will work it out for their good. You Lord will turn it around in their favor and save many lives. You Lord can and will, not only do it for their sakes, but for Your glory. So I speak Shalom! Peace! Nothing broken, nothing lacking, wholeness, completeness, and prosperity, in Jesus name. Amen!

Sit and reflect. How have you allowed God to use you even when you were in a broken state.

Being confident of this very thing, that he which hath begun a good work in you will perform it until the day of Jesus Christ.
Philippians 1:6 KJV

For I know the thoughts that I think toward you, saith the LORD, thoughts of peace, and not of evil, to give you an expected end.
Jeremiah 29:11 KJV

The Romans Road To Salvation

Romans 3:23
For All have sinned and come short of the glory of God.

Roman 6:23
For the wages of sin is death, but the gift of God is eternal life through Christ Jesus our Lord.

Romans 10:9-10
That if thou shalt confess with thy mouth the Lord Jesus and shalt believe in thine heart that God hath raised Him from the dead, thou shalt be saved.
For with the heart man believeth unto righteousness; and with the mouth confession is made unto salvation.

Roman 10:13
For whoever shall call upon the name of the Lord shall be saved.

The Prodigal
My Story, His Glory!

I was that prodigal! For a long time I didn't know who I was. Let me clarify! I was born into a two parent home. I had a mother and a father and four siblings. I knew my grandparents, my aunts, uncles and cousins. We grew up celebrating holidays together, having big Sunday dinners with extended family and playing outdoors in the neighborhood with other kids until after the street lights came on. I was a playful talkative kid who loved being outdoors in the hot summer sun. I remember using my bare feet to pop the tar bubbles that would bubble up on our street from the scorching summer heat. I loved school and learning, my teachers, my friends and the fact that I had siblings to play with as well.

As far back as I can remember I would have dreams when I slept. In fact, my earliest memory is a dream. It was always a dark lonely dream of me being alone in a small dark space. I would look around and no one else was there. It was just me alone with my knees up to my chest, my arms wrapped around them and a feeling of loneliness. It was a reoccurring dream. Yet, at that particular time in my life the dream did not reflect who I was outwardly because I loved my family, loved school, loved to talk, play and have fun.

I gave my life to the LORD at age eleven I was baptized on a Sunday, April 1st, in the name of the Father, Son and Holy Ghost at the baptist church in our neighborhood. Happy and excited about my decision, I told everybody. So my journey with God began.

As a teen, for some reason, I began to feel those reoccurring dreams of loneliness reflecting in my own life. I began to feel lost and out of place like I didn't belong anywhere. I didn't know it then but I know now that around adolescence many teens begin to feel this way. This is due mostly to hormones, changes taking place in their bodies and peer pressure. The reoccurring dreams I was having only heightened those feelings. I felt like a square peg trying to fit into a round hole and it **just ... wasn't... working!**...

Thus, my teen and young adult years were a *'testing of the waters'* so to speak. That feeling of being different and not fitting in began to show in my behavior, as I did everything I was bad enough to do. I was disobedient, I became a terrible liar, I talked back and became disrespectful to a certain point. I say a certain point because I knew there was a boundary I had better not cross. My mother didn't take to disrespect kindly. Had I said anything too far out of line or blatant, I would have found myself waking up from a coma off the floor. I experimented with drugs lightly. I smoked a joint every now and then; and once I tried to do a hard drug. I was a lightweight. I was green to that kind of stuff and I knew it was addictive so I never did it again. Drugs were not for me. Even now, I rarely even take prescription drugs that are prescribed to me by my doctor. Simply because I don't like the side effects.

I tried hard to to belong and discover who I was. I wanted to get rid of those lost and lonely feelings of never belonging. The desire to fit in was so persistent. It's hard to explain if you've never been there and never felt the emptiness of trying to fill a void in life.

I knew this wasn't me. The sex, the drugs, and the partying didn't feel right! And I still never really quite fit in anyway. Yet, I kept trying to be someone I wasn't and hang with people who I was never meant to be a part of. I ignored the voice of the Father when I heard Him call and say to me, **"I'm still here, you can come home"**. But I was trying to find the answers to those questions like, Who am I? What am I doing here? What am I supposed to be doing? I want the loneliness to go away! I truly felt lost and as if I didn't belong anywhere. My mom soon began calling me her 'strange' child. I had just stopped talking! I can remember in grade school, the fifth or sixth grades my parents would go to the parent teacher conferences and the teacher would always compliment my "A" work in the classroom and willingness to participate, but they always had a problem with me talking too much. They said I was a disturbance to the other children. Then my mom would chime in, *"She is just like her father. They always have to be the center of attention."* And one year that statement hit me different. It entered a deep part of my soul and it began to take root and grow. I thought if she didn't like

this part of my dad, she didn't like this part of me. I didn't talk much after that and she noticed it. But Instead of asking me what was wrong, she just began to say, *"You're my strange child. You don't talk. It's no fun going anywhere with you."* That hurt even more. The strain from that time didn't remain however; partly because I pushed that pain down and later decided to forgive and move on.

My desire to have friends and fit in drew me away from God and I was moonwalking my way right into hell. I was putting a greater and greater distance between me and God and one day I looked back. Having now totally turned my back to him with a huge cavern between us, I could no longer see him and I could only faintly hear His still small voice saying, **"Repent! Come back to me."** Yet, even in my sin, God showed me mercy and extended His grace that He gave to me time after time to get it right. But where sin abounded, grace did much more abound. (Romans 5:20)

Often, during that time of sin and running, I would think: "If the Lord were to return right now, I would be lost forever". I thought God would blot my name from His book according to Exodus 32:32. I knew I had to make things right between me and the Lord. And so, just like the story of the prodigal son, in the book of Luke chapter 15, God extended His grace toward me. He pulled back the lie and deception the devil had covering my eyes, just long enough for me to **'come to myself'** like the prodigal son did. I lifted up my eyes to heaven and prayed, *"I've made a mess of this! Besides my husband and my children, nothing has turned out right. Father I know that you have better for me. I know with You I can do better than this."* And with that, I went home. I repented, and asked the Lord for forgiveness. I re-dedicated my life back to Jesus and just as I'd hoped, He was still there waiting with His arms wide open. And where our journey had stopped all those years before, it began again; forward and upward. I got into a good church, began praying and reading the Word, and teaching it to my kids. I learned of my calling and gifts.

Prophets prophesied to me and told me that I'm an Intercessor, one who God speaks to in dreams and visions; a teacher with healing in my hands. I began learning who I was in Christ (actually

still learning) and what my purpose is here on earth, which is to worship and praise

God and let my light so shine that others would see and glorify the God of Heaven. (Matthew 5:16)

This is what was missing from my early days in Christ. This is what I didn't know; that a person has to be taught and God gives grace. Instead I heard and believed the lies of the enemy. I let those lies dictate who I became; an exact opposite of who the Lord said I was and was called to be in Him. Satan said I was loud, that I talked too much, that I was a liar, that I would never amount to anything, that I would turn out to be just like other family members who turned to drugs and got pregnant as teenagers, that I wasn't good enough, and that there was something wrong with me; his lies said hide! Never be seen! And I let him steal my voice, silence me, and steal my joy and passion.

After rededicating my life back to the Lord as I stated above, I began to search and learn my true identity in Christ and who He says that I am. Everyday I make the conscientious choice to believe the truth of the
Word of God which is helping me to heal from the wounds of my past, deliver me and drown out the voice and the lies of the enemy. In the Word of God, Jesus says:

I am Loved,
I am blessed,
I am chosen,
I am adopted,
I am redeemed,
I am forgiven,
I am saved,
I am called,

I am the workmanship of God according Ephesians chapters 2 & 3; I am fearfully and wonderfully made according to Psalm 139. I am an heir and Joint heir with Christ according to Romans 8:17. If the Son therefore shall make you free, ye shall be free indeed, according to John 8:36.

Jesus says that I am no longer condemned, "For there is therefore no condemnation to those who are in Christ Jesus." (Romans 8:1)

You see, the Lord never left me, I left Him. I left the safety and the covering of my home in the Lord. His word says that He is married to the backslider (Jeremiah 3:14). He is in covenant with us and He will never break His covenant and there is nothing we can do to separate ourselves from His love (Romans 8). So, my story, I tell for His Glory. My story, I tell in the hopes that someone will identify and say, "If God did that for her, then I believe He'll do it for me." My story, I tell it to give hope and to point in the direction of Jesus. Although it may not be so bad compared to others who have gone through some horrific and tragic life situations, it's my story. It is uniquely me, and maybe it's not so different from some of yours. But we all have a story to tell. And His love is big enough, all encompassing and unfailing enough to love and welcome you home, whether it be for the first time or the fiftieth, no questions asked. What the enemy meant for evil, the Lord will and has turned it around for my good and yours. Nothing is lost or wasted with God. He can and will use everything that you go through to teach you and grow you and strengthen you to be used to help others and glorify Him.

So if you were to ask me now who I am, I would say, "I am a child of God, loved and rejoiced over with my name securely written in the Lamb's book of Life." Am I lonely? No! Not any more! Because I talk to Him everyday. I tell Him everything and I know He listens. At times, He has answered prayers for me so fast it makes my head spin; lol in a good way :-) I love Him and He knows that. He knows me better than I know myself and He is yet teaching me and showing me, *'Me'* and more of Him and I am learning to enjoy our journey together.

So, my question to you is, Are you're tired of being in your mess? Are you tired of feeling like you're all alone? If you've tried it your way and messed up royally; you've sown your wild oats, got it out of your system, or not! Burned too many bridges and you're

simply tired of running. The Father says, **"Son/Daughter, It's time to come home."** Won't you come?

I've heard it said that the angels rejoice over one sinner when they come to the Lord. I choose to believe they also rejoice when a wayward son or daughter returns home. **Let's celebrate!**

Father, forgive me! I repent of my sins and I want to come home. I renounce my life of sin and I accept your free salvation and the safety of your loving arms and shelter. I ask for Your Holy Spirit to come and dwell in me and teach me your ways and how to love you. In Jesus name I pray. Amen

What's your decision today? Do you reside safely in the dwelling place with God? If no, what are you going to do? If yes, what can or will you do to bring someone else into safety with you?

_____

_____

_____

_____

_____

_____

_____

_____

_____

_____

_____

_____

_____

_____

_____

_____

_____

_____

_____

_____

But seek ye first the kingdom of God, and His righteousness: and all these things shall be added unto you. Matthew 6:33 KJV

And ye shall seek me, and find me, when ye shall search for me with all your heart. Jeremiah 29:13 KJV

KING OF KINGS & LORD OF LORDS

...SURELY I COME

QUICKLY.

AMEN

EVEN SO, COME, LORD JESUS

Love Song

One day while in worship, I heard the Lord speak the words, **"Love Song"**. The Lord said to me that He has given each of us a **Love Song** that He placed within each of us and He wants us to sing that **love song** back to Him in worship.

Just as He dropped these words into my spirit, our worship leader began to sing a **Song of the Lord** as the Spirit gave him utterance. This I took as confirmation of what the Lord had just given me.
I went and told my pastor that I had just received a word from the Lord that I think He wanted me to share. After our worship, but before the sermon, the pastor gave me the microphone and I began to share how just moments before, the Lord dropped the words **Love Song** into my spirit. He explained to me we each have a **love song** He has placed within each of us, as individual as our fingerprints a **love song** we are to sing unto Him.

We are to sing with our hearts;
Sing with our mouths;
Sing with our lives totally surrendered to Him.
We are to sing the **love song** He has ordained within each of us.
The Lord says to open your hearts to me and sing!
Open your mouths to me and sing!
Surrender your lives to me in holiness and righteousness and let your lives sing the beautiful **love song** within you.

Our Lord loves the sound of your voice in worship and praise and prayer unto Him. It doesn't matter how badly you think you may sound; The Most High loves the way your voice sounds. When you praise, worship, adore, magnify and exalt Him; it's beautiful to Him. The Song of Solomon Passion translation chapter 2 v/13-14:

13.Can you not discern this new day of destiny breaking forth around you? The early signs of my purposes and plans are bursting forth. The budding vines of new life are now blooming everywhere. The fragrance of their flowers whispers, "There is change in the air." Arise, my love, my beautiful companion, and

run with me to the higher place. For now is the time to arise and come away with me.

      14.For you are my dove, hidden in the split-open rock. It was I who took you and hid you up high in the secret stairway of the sky. Let me see your radiant face and hear your sweet voice. How beautiful your eyes of worship and lovely your voice in prayer.

Psalm 96:1
O sing unto the Lord a new song: sing unto the Lord, all the earth. KJV

Psalm 40:3
And He hath put a new song in my mouth, even praise unto our God: many shall see it and fear, and shall trust in the Lord, Amen. KJV

Sing your song unto the Lord!
Hear it in your spirit. Write it down; record it. Do whatever you need to do, however He gives it to you and **sing unto the Lord your new song.**

_____
_____
_____
_____
_____
_____
_____
_____
_____
_____
_____
_____
_____
_____
_____
_____
_____
_____
_____
_____

And this is the promise that he hath promised us, even eternal life.
1 John 2:25 KJV

God is my strength and power: and he maketh my way perfect.
2 Samuel 22:33 KJV

Pray for the Nations

Psalm 150

1. Praise ye the Lord. Praise God in his sanctuary: praise him in the firmament of his power.

2. Praise him for his mighty acts: praise him according to his excellent greatness.

3. Praise him with the sound of the trumpet: praise him with the psaltery and harp.

4. Praise him with the timbrel and dance: praise him with stringed instruments and organs.

5. Praise him upon the loud cymbals: praise him upon the high sounding cymbals.

6. Let every thing that hath breath praise the Lord. Praise ye the Lord. KJV

HOPE

There are some reading this that are losing hope, or have already lost hope. I feel it in my spirit for some of you.
You've been beat up by the world.
You've put your trust in people instead of God:
>Family, Husband or Wife,
>Career or Money, Church,
>Apostle or Pastor

And they have all let you down or disappointed you in some way or another. The Lord impressed upon my heart to let you know right now that HE, the LORD Jesus Christ is renewing and restoring your HOPE. He is where your trust should be and He wants you to know that He is restoring and renewing your Hope: only believe; only receive.

Trust in the Lord with all of your heart, and lean not unto your own understanding; in all your ways acknowledge Him and He shall direct your paths. (Proverbs 3:5-6 KJV)

Or maybe you've trusted in God, prayed and prayed, but haven't seen the manifestation or answer to your prayers. This is a season of Hope fulfilled. The Lord says don't give up!
Don't get weary in well doing for in due season you shall reap if you faint not. This is the season of Hope fulfilled. He will show Himself strong in your life. His help is on the way.
The way He gave it to me within the first couple months of 2020 is **UPGRADE**. As I was driving, not sure of what song on the radio I was listening to, the Holy Spirit interrupted my thoughts and said **UPGRADE!**
As He continued to expound, He said that His people will get upgrades. They will get promotions and bonuses in the Spirit meaning Power. He said that just because we are His sons and daughters; because we Believe, we would be endowed with **more.** More of His Spirit; more of His power, more Hope; more Faith and that it would be known by all; that a distinction would be seen and known. The way the Holy Spirit made me to further understand was this:
>You work for a company and it's end of the year and bonus time. Back in the day when American companies still paid bonuses, you got a bonus on your end of the year check. You

received extra from the profits made throughout the year if the company shared its profits with its employees and not just its shareholders. And simply because you work for the company, no matter how long you've been with them, you shared in the blessing.

So Just Hold On!

Encourage yourself in the Lord as David had to do at times in his life."And David was greatly distressed; for the people spake of stoning him, because the soul of all the people was grieved, every man for his sons and daughter: but David encouraged himself in the LORD his God. (1 Samuel 30:6 KJV)

For we are saved by **HOPE**: but **HOPE** that is seen is not **HOPE**: for what a man seeth, why doth he yet HOPE for? But if we **HOPE** for that we see not, then do we with patience wait for it. (Romans 8:24-25 KJV)

Therefore my heart is glad, and my glory rejoices: my flesh also shall rest in Hope." (Psalm 16:9 KJV)

Be of good courage, and He shall strengthen your heart, all ye that hope in the LORD. (Psalm 31:24 KJV)

But I will hope continually, and will yet praise thee more and more. (Psalm 71:14 KJV)

HOPE!
FAITH BELIEF TRUST CONFIDENCE
His Help is on the way
Put your **HOPE** in the LORD!

Father I pray that you will let your son or daughter know in some meaningful and tangible way that you love them and that they are the most precious thing in the world to you right now. Show them through your Word that you can be trusted above all men and that you have only the best in store for them now and in their future. Show them your heart and teach them to search for your heart in all things so that they may never be disappointed again by man, but will only look to you. In Jesus name I pray, Amen.

And the peace of God, which passeth all understanding, shall keep your hearts and minds through Christ Jesus. Philippians 4:7 KJV

God is love; and he that dwelleth in love dwelleth in God, and God in him. 1 John 4:16 KJV

AND GOD SAID

Let there be light
Forcefully, He said into the night
No longer void, shapeless and without form
In OUR form, In OUR image, let us create
So created WE them

God's plan from the start
O such a genius work of art
With the choice that He gave us
We chose wrong - we chose not

We chose not to obey
we chose not to take heed
The still small voice of our God
Instead we let that snake, that lying
Snake plant a seed

A seed of doubt
A seed of disbelief
A seed that cost us our lives
A seed that grows only weeds

But Yahweh the True God
Not caught unaware
He put His plan into action
Jesus would come to trip the snare

God came in the form of a baby
Born in poverty and shame
A star announced His Holy birth
Our Savior our Redeemer
Our God had come to earth

But He was not what we thought
He brought peace, we wanted war
He taught love, patience, turn the other cheek
Turn the other cheek, don't use the sword

We mocked Him, we scorned, we lied, and we schemed
We devised, we plotted, we planned
His demise, we must succeed

He must die we said
Be silenced - teach no more
For He teaches a doctrine that puts us to shame
He teaches a doctrine that exalts His name

That name Jesus, who knew
The carpenter's son?
No Jesus-The Son of the Most Holy One!

Emmanuel - God is with us
Yeshua - our Salvation- Messiah, Prince of Peace
Our Deliverer has come
He's come to meet our every need

But again we chose wrong
We err'd in our own way
We ignored His voice again
We chose His death, He must die we'd say

Found guilty we tried Him
We hung Him on a tree
That cross brutal and bloody
Not realizing He was doing this for me?

His eyes, even through the pain
bore so much love
With every crack of the whip
I heard Him whisper,
He whispered my name

We stretched Him up high

We stretched Him up wide
For me He hung His head
For me, for me, He died?

Why did I not see it?
How did I not know?
He was gentle, loving and kind
He healed so many, so many he fed
He told the lame to get up, get up and take your bed
He told the blinded eye - SEE!
and with only His voice He raised the dead

Now the sky is so very dark
The veil has been torn
He cried "It is finished"

O why did I mock Him?
Why did I scorn?

He came to save the lost
He came to set me free
To loose my bands and chains
He came for all to receive

So now I cry What must I do?
What must I do to be saved?
I don't want to go down
into a dark, stanky grave

Repent! Repent!
I once heard Him say
Repent! Repent!
For the Kingdom of heaven is at hand

So on my knees I do now bow
With my tongue I do confess
That Jesus is Lord! Jesus is Lord!

I now pour out
I now give Him my best

And you too can have this Savior
You too can have Him as Lord
God's perfect gift to the world
Born on that first Christmas morn

But in the grave He did not stay
3 days, 3 night, that was all
He got up! He got up from the grave
He got up and redeemed us all

He's very soon to return
With all victory, glory and might
Behold I come quickly He says
I come quickly, be ready day or night

For I AM the root and Offspring of David
I AM the Bright and Morning Star
I AM the Alpha and Omega
The First and the Last
I AM the Beginning and the End
I AM The Great, The Great I AM!

For the wages of sin is death, but the gift of God is eternal life.
Romans 6:23 KJV

And of some have compassion, making a difference. Jude 1:22 KJV

HEAVENLY PERSPECTIVE

Ephesians 2:6, "And hath raised us up together and made us sit together in heavenly places in Christ Jesus." KJV

Have you ever had a though hit you from out of nowhere? It's like voila! And it's simply there and you wonder, "Why have I never seen this before?" This happened to me while reading Ephesians 2:6 one day; all of a sudden I got it. I understood from where I was waging battle in the spirit realm and my prayers shifted.

We fight from a place of offense; gaining new territory and victory.
We fight from a place of victory; because Christ has never lost a battle.
We fight from a high place being seated with Him.
We don't fight from a place of defense, because God is never caught off guard.
We don't fight from a place of defeat because Christ has never been defeated.

God always advances us forward to take and conquer the land. When we have the wrong perspective, we're on the defense, we're reactive, our sight is limited or blocked. But what the Holy Spirit revealed to me that day was as a child of God seated with Jesus Christ in heavenly places on the right hand of the Father, when we war against the enemy from our heavenly seat, our sight is limitless. We now have a vantage point that see the whole landscape: our perspective is changed.

In my minds eye I see a barnyard chicken that can only see the things around her at ground level. She spends a great deal of time pecking at the ground to get sustenance; never having the need or opportunity to spread her wings to full capacity and fly. But I also see an eagle in flight: wings fully extended catching the wind and soaring high above the trees and above the clouds where with her eagle eyes she can see everything from all directions and land in the cleft of a rock high upon a mountain top where it makes it's nest.

The Lord told me then that he was changing our perspective. He was changing how we saw things in our lives, our circumstances,

things in the spirit and things in the natural. No longer will we see ourselves defeated, oppressed, downtrodden, last or forgotten, but we and others will see and recognize the Christ, the anointing within ourselves and each other and we will celebrate one another. The enemy has made His children almost go into hiding. God's children are silent when they should be speaking. God's children are lifeless when they should be on the move full of fire, energy and momentum. God is changing this: He is changing our perspective. We will know it, we will see it. The shift has already begun.

My prayers shifted as I began to pray
from **victory**,
from **it's already done** and
from **It is so!**

I began to see how as I prayed from heavenly places looking down, seeing the enemy beneath me and being able to see with a 360 degree radius as long as I stay in Christ, and as long as I prayed believing, victory is promised, victory is guaranteed.

1 Corinthians 15:57 KJV
But thanks be to God, which giveth us the victory through our Lord Jesus Christ.

2 Corinthians 2:14 KJV
Now thanks be unto God, which always causeth us to triumph in Christ, and maketh manifest the savor of His knowledge by us in every place.

**Where are you seated?
What is your perspective?
How is it reflected in your prayers?**

Seeing then that we have a great high priest, that is passed into the heavens, Jesus the Son of God, let us hold fast our profession.

Hebrews 4:14 KJV

But the word of the Lord endureth forever... 1 Peter 1:25 KJV

Now faith is the substance of things hoped for, the evidence of things not seen. Hebrews 11:1 KJV

...And God is able to make all grace abound toward you; that ye, always having all sufficiency in all things, may abound to every good work,
2 Cor 5:8 KJV

AT THE END OF IT ALL

I was recently watching a movie call "Draft Day" a movie released in 2014 starring Kevin Costner. At the beginning of this movie Kevin writes a little note to himself and sticks it in his pants pocket. As the movies goes on periodically he pulls that note out and looks. All the while, the audience, if they were anything like me, wondered, "What is written on that piece of paper?"

Well, as the movie nears the end, the big draft day is here and excitement and stress are at an all time high. Wheeling and dealing is going on and one can hardly stand it when the least expectant thing happens; Kevin's character as the General Manager of the Cleveland Browns, on his NFL turn to choose who he wants for his team passes up the #1 draft pick for another promising young player with heart and passion, Vontae Mack played by Chadwick Boseman, who was barely on the radar of the other general managers. Needless to say, this throws everyone in a tizzy. What is wrong with the #1 draft pick? Why did Kevin pass him up? More behind the scene trading and shifting goes on and what was thought to be #1 is now #8 or so and what was thought to be less valuable was thrusted to the #1 position and the Cleveland Browns came out not only better during that draft, but for three years to come.

I bring up this movie because watching it revealed a couple of things to me.
1. When you know that you've heard from God, make the right choice and be obedient to His voice.
Have faith in your decision and stick to it. See, what Kevin wrote on that small piece of paper early that morning was what he knew was the right decision. He wrote, "No matter what, pick Vontae Mack". He had to write himself a note to remind himself throughout the day of his decision and not to let the 'other' voices of doubt and disbelief and questioning distract him, nor deter him from what he knew was the right choice and what was good for the team.

2. God can take what looks like an awful situation and turn it around for your good.

Through out the day, Kevin's character was doubting himself and his abilities, and this led to him accepting a terrible deal that would give a rival team his number one picks for the next three seasons. This was awful! He knew it, but now didn't see how he could get out of this bad deal.

But God...

Later that day he got some information that turned out to be priceless. He now had information that other teams didn't have and he relied on his gut instinct. But to us, the Believers, we rely on the Holy Spirit. He turned a bad deal that would affect him, his reputation as a general manager and his team into a win for the next three years and more.

God promotes! Vonte Mack moved from the back of the line to the front of the line. You may think that you have been forgotten. You may think that what you have to offer is too small and that you are just a nobody: "What can I do?" But God may say and think differently. God can and will suddenly, and unexpectedly move you to the forefront. God has the final say.

If you put your trust and life in God's hands, HE will make you privy to information from the Spirit realm and give you the upper hand over the enemy and their plans. HE will give you wisdom to make right decisions, strategy to outwit the devil and words of wisdom; instructions on how to make a thing work and be successful. And what looked bad, God has now turned it around for your good.

God showed me that my time with HIM, in the quiet of the day - for me is the first thing in the morning before everyone else gets up - when I spend time with Him in prayer and silence and with the Word before me, HE speaks. And what HE speaks I can take that to the bank as the saying goes, because it is true and spot on and it will not return to Him void. These quiet moments are vital. They ground you and ensure your footing on the Rock, the solid foundation which is Jesus Christ and no matter what comes at you throughout the day; whether lies from the enemy, doubt in yourself, the voices of well-meaning family and friends and the

noise and chatter that each day can bring. Even if it means writing yourself an actual note to stick in your pocket. "AT THE END OF IT ALL, let your decision be for Jesus Christ and to trust and stick with HIM.

Father I thank you for the moments of quietness and stillness in Your presence. I thank You that you are always speaking, and always willing to give wisdom and insight to your children. I thank you that you never leave us unawares, nor will you let us walk into a snare or trap. You give us warning and all we have to do is get in your presence. Lord help those needing to discipline themselves in this area. Let them tangibly feel your wooing and drawing to us by your love, your kindness, your presence, peace, warmth and goodness that will keep them coming back. Your Word says you are faithful and that you watch over your Word to perform it and that you can do ALL things but fail nor do you lie. So I thank you for your promises and the fulfillment of each one. I thank you that **'AT THE END OF IT ALL'** we will have made the right decision to **"PICK JESUS CHRIST NO MATTER WHAT"**.

For our God is a consuming fire. Hebrews 12:29 KJV

That ye might walk worthy of the Lord unto all pleasing, being fruitful in every good work, and increasing in the knowledge of God.
Colossians 1:10 KJV

Faith is our Key, our Access

to

Healings

Miracles, Sign & Wonders

THE SPIRIT OF THE FEAR OF THE LORD

The fear of the Lord according to the bible:

Fear or Holy Reverence
Respect
Honor
Adoration
Awe and wonder!

The fear of the Lord, that is wisdom - Job 28:28
The fear of the Lord is clean - Psalm 19:9
The fear of the Lord is the beginning of wisdom - Psalm 111:10
The fear of the Lord is the beginning of knowledge - Proverbs 1:7
The fear of the Lord is prolonged days - Proverbs 10:27
The fear of the Lord hates evil, pride, arrogance, the evil way and the froward mouth - Proverbs 8:13
The fear of the Lord is strong confidence - Proverbs 14:26
The fear of the Lord is a fountain of life - Proverbs 14:27
The fear of the Lord is the instruction of wisdom - Proverb 15:33
The fear of the Lord, men depart from evil - Proverbs 16:6
The fear of the Lord tends to life - Proverbs 19:23
The fear of the Lord is riches, honor and life - Proverbs 22:4
The fear of the Lord is treasure - Isaiah 33:16

And the spirit of the LORD shall rest upon him, the spirit of wisdom and understanding, the spirit of counsel and might, the spirit of knowledge and of the fear of the LORD. Isaiah 11:2 KJV

According to these scriptures, the fear of the LORD is good. I mean who wouldn't want wisdom, prolonged life, not just confidence, but strong confidence, riches, honor, and treasures?

But we've lost the **Spirit of the fear of the Lord**!

We've gotten complacent
unaware
uninformed
prideful
conceited
desirous of vain-glory
asleep

We've made the LORD, like a little idol god to be put upon a shelf for display, but never used or called upon until we're really in dire need.

We've made Him common
lack of privilege or special status
second rate
elementary.

THESE THINGS OUGHT NOT BE!
He is GOD!

The Most High God the Maker of the universe and ALL that is therein
El Shaddai WAS before anything and shall ALWAYS be EVERYTHING seen and unseen Elohim created

We are so casual with Him. We are so careless. Yes, I too have sinned in this area and must repent: forgive me LORD! And He is so loving, gracious, merciful, gentle and long-suffering. We tend to forget, He is the ONE who has all the time in this known universe. He created time. We're the ones living on borrowed time.

Isaiah 29:13 KJV
"Wherefore the Lord said, forasmuch as this people draw near me with their mouth, and with their lips do honor me, but have removed their heart far from me, and their fear toward me is taught by the precept of men:"

This is also referenced in Matthew 15:8 and Mark 7:6

The state of our hearts have waxed cold. We have forgotten our first love: Revelation 2:4 KJV "Nevertheless I have somewhat against thee, because thou hast left thy first love."

 I DESIRE YOUR HEARTS! BRING ME YOUR HEARTS!

The Holy Spirit woke me up one morning with these words, "Give God your Best! That just kept resonating in my spirit over and over again. Even after I woke up, "Give God your best!" was all I could think about. I asked the questions, "Have I not been giving Him my best already? What is my best? How do I give that to Him if I don't know what that is?" Those words and the questions they generated in my mind left me feeling low and defeated. I had already begun to feel weary. I had no fight left in me to even pray against the enemy. And the enemy was telling me that prayer was too hard, too laborious, and takes too long and too much effort to get into the presence of God. I listened and couldn't pray. The Lord put on my heart to call a fellow intercessor and have her pray with me. I said to myself that I would call her that evening. Evening came and although I had every intention on calling her just as He said to do, she called me first. I silently said, "Thank you God." About midway through the call I told her that I had planned on calling her that night, but God made sure we connected and HE had you call me first. I told her what I was going through and how I was feeling. She said it sounds like you are in a 'dry season'. She then went on to explain that a dry season is when you get to a place where the things of God seem redundant and ordinary. It's when you don't know how to pray or what to pray for. It's when you're tired and weary in your spirit and soul; things have become 'dry'. I told her that sounds about right. That is some of what I'm feeling and going through. She asked me if I had time to pray. I said "yes".

I truly did and it was exactly what I needed and wanted at the time. We began to pray in the spirit and we prayed with the understanding. We prayed for each other and we prayed for other saints. We prayed for lost souls to find God and we prayed for our children and all children in general. We prayed! And before we knew it an hour and a half almost two hours had passed. But when we said our good nights, we both testified of the release we felt and thanked God for sending His ministering angels. It felt good and I knew in my spirit that I had gotten some deliverance that night. Yet, the following day, something still nagged at me. I felt I needed something more. I texted two more intercessors from back home and asked them to pray for me in their quiet time with the Lord. One sister wrote back and told me that in times like these, she gets before the LORD and simply pours out her heart. It's not necessarily a formal prayer, but a simple heart to heart, pouring out of my soul to God. Our time together (mine and the Lord's) that morning was so intimate and I had such an encounter with God. I cried so deeply. It was so cleansing. I prayed:

***Psalm 51** 1. Have mercy upon me, O God, according to thy lovingkindness: according unto the multitude of thy tender mercies blot out my transgressions. 2 Wash me throughly from mine iniquity, and cleanse me from my sin. 3 For I acknowledge my transgressions: and my sin is ever before me. 4 Against thee, thee only, have I sinned, and done this evil in thy sight: that thou mightest be justified when thou speakest, and be clear when thou judgest. 5 Behold, I was shapen in iniquity; and in sin did my mother conceive me. 6 Behold, thou desirest truth in the inward parts: and in the hidden part thou shalt make me to know wisdom. 7 Purge me with hyssop, and I shall be clean: wash me, and I shall be whiter than snow. 8 Make me to hear joy and gladness; that the bones which thou hast broken may rejoice. 9 Hide thy face from my sins, and blot out all mine iniquities. 10 Create in me a clean heart, O God; and renew a right spirit within me. 11 Cast me not away from thy presence; and take not thy holy spirit from me. 12 Restore unto me the joy of thy salvation; and uphold me with*

thy free spirit. 13 Then will I teach transgressors thy ways; and sinners shall be converted unto thee. 14 Deliver me from blood guiltiness, O God, thou God of my salvation: and my tongue shall sing aloud of thy righteousness. 15 O Lord, open thou my lips; and my mouth shall shew forth thy praise. 16 For thou desirest not sacrifice; else would I give it: thou delightest not in burnt offering. 17 The sacrifices of God are a broken spirit: a broken and a contrite heart, O God, thou wilt not despise. 18 Do good in thy good pleasure unto Zion: build thou the walls of Jerusalem. 19 Then shalt thou be pleased with the sacrifices of righteousness, with burnt offering and whole burnt offering: then shall they offer bullocks upon thine altar.

At the end of our encounter, I needed to repent and ask for forgiveness. The Lord showed me my heart with a couple of examples and this is how HE did it. He said, "You know how first thing in the morning when you begin to brew your pot of coffee for yourself and your husband? I said,"Yes Lord!" He said, "You know how you like to get the first cup of the freshly brewed coffee when the pot is about a quarter of the way full? I said, "Yes Lord!" He said, That cup to you is the BEST cup of coffee out of the entire pot. That cup is the most flavorful and most enjoyable cup of coffee to you. It's what makes the coffee worth drinking." Yes God! I said. "That is what I want from you. I want the BEST, the first, the most flavorful and most enjoyable part of you." This hit home for me because I am a coffee drinker; you hear me! He said, "Give me your BEST!" The Lord showed me that my heart toward Him was not quite right. In my heart I did not put Him first and foremost. You know how you say within yourself to the Lord, (after this Lord, I'll read Your word. After I get done with this, I'll make time to pray, Lord). I kept giving Him excuses why I couldn't drop everything when He called to me and be obedient and do as He asked. My heart, my attitude toward Him was fitting Him in when I could, instead of fitting my day in around Him. He took me to the book of Genesis to read the story of Cain and Able. Abel's offering was acceptable to God and respected, but Cain's offering was not. Why? As I reread the passages, the Bible says in **Genesis 4:1** *And Adam knew Eve his wife; and she conceived,*

*and bare Cain, and said, I have gotten a man from the Lord. **2** And she again bare his brother Abel. And Abel was a keeper of sheep, but Cain was a tiller of the ground. **3** And in process of time it came to pass, that Cain brought of the fruit of the ground an offering unto the Lord. **4** And Abel, he also brought of the firstlings of his flock and of the fat thereof. And the Lord had respect unto Abel and to his offering: **5** But unto Cain and to his offering he had not respect.* See the difference? Able's offering it says was of the firstling of his flock and the fat thereof. Meaning Able brought the choicest. His offering was a real sacrifice because he chose to give to God the number one choice of animals in his flock and his heart toward God was of true reverence. Cain's offering on the other hand had no differentiating statements. It simply says Cain brought of the fruit of the ground an offering: nothing special about it at all. It wasn't the first fruit of his harvest or yield. It wasn't the juiciest, the finest or choicest of barley or wheat of fruit or vegetables. It doesn't sound like Cain's heart was into his offering unto the Lord at all. There was no real sacrifice from Cain. It almost feels as if Cain may have said, "Let me hurry and get this offering over with." The passage goes on to say, **5** *And Cain was very wroth, and his countenance fell.* **6** *And the Lord said unto Cain, Why art thou wroth? And why is thy countenance fallen?* **7** *If thou doest well, shalt thou not be accepted? And if thou doest not well, sin lies at the door. And unto thee shall be his desire, and thou shalt rule over him.* **8** *And Cain talked with Abel his brother: and it came to pass, when they were in the field, that Cain rose up against Abel his brother, and slew him.* I saw where my heart was. I saw what I was doing. God the Father in His gentle and loving way showed me; corrected me. (Proverbs 3:12) The book of Proverbs 3:9 also says, *"Honor the Lord with thy substance and with the **first fruits** of **ALL** thine increase."* I understand this to mean my time, my talents, my treasure: everything! I am making adjustments even as I write this to make sure I put and keep The One and Only True God in His proper place at head and first giving my BEST to Him in my heart and in my actions to Him at all times.

So **COME BACK!** The Lord says. "Bring me your **HEARTS to the altar. Make your hearts altars unto me!** Sacred! Holy! I desire your hearts first. Why our hearts? The bible says that man looks

on the outward appearance, but God looks at the heart. (1 Samuel 16:7) In our physical bodies the heart is the muscle that keeps every other muscle and organ in the body running because it's the heart that PUMPS the vital life source (our blood) through every part of our body - the life sustaining blood we can't do without. The Bible says in Leviticus 17:11 & 14 "For the life of the flesh is in the blood." Also emotionally, the heart is where we feel pain, hurt, joy, happiness, sorrow; everything emotional. Sometimes we make decisions based on our hearts and not our minds. If you can capture someones heart, it can and will override the mind almost every time. So why wouldn't God want our hearts? It is the epicenter so to say, of the human being. Give me your hearts God says, and if He has our hearts everything else will follow. Let me burn away ALL that is not like me with my Holy Fire. Let me transform you and make you new by replacing your hearts of stone with hearts of flesh. Ezekiel 11:19 & Ezekiel 36:26

If my people which are called by my name, shall humble themselves, and pray, and seek my face, and turn from their wicked ways; then will I hear from heaven, and will forgive their sin, and will heal their land. 2 Chronicles 7:14 KJV

Prayer
Forgive us Father! Forgive us LORD for making You common and ordinary. Forgive us for forgetting our first love. Forgive us for not offering You our BEST; our first! Turn the hearts of Your people and this nation back toward You LORD. For it is only by Your Spirit that this can be done. We ask You to give us hearts that are pure toward You, hearts of flesh, hearts of compassion, hearts that burn and hunger for You and You only. Turn our hearts toward You Father so that we always offer You our BEST. The best of us. A real living sacrifice which is our reasonable service. In Jesus name I pray, Amen.

Where is the Lord in your life? Examine your heart today. What can you start doing today to make sure that God is first and that you give Him your BEST at all times?

_____

_____

_____

_____

_____

_____

_____

_____

_____

_____

_____

_____

_____

_____

_____

_____

_____

_____

_____

Put on the whole armor of God, that ye may be able to stand against the wiles of the devil. Ephesians 6:11 KJV

Finally, brethren, whats ever things are true, whatsoever things are honest, whatsoever things are just, whatsoever things are pure, whats ever things are lovely, whatsoever things are of good report; if there be any virtue and if there be any praise, think on these things.
Philippians 4:8 KJV

Our Father
Who art in heaven,
Hallowed be thy name
Thy Kingdom come
Thy will be done
In earth as it is in heaven
Give us this day
Our daily bread
and forgive us our debts,
As we forgive our debtors
And lead us not into temptation
But deliver us from evil
For thine is the Kingdom
And the power,
And the glory,
For ever
Amen.

Surely Goodness and Mercy

Psalm 23:6
"Surely goodness and mercy shall follow me all the days of my life and I will dwell in the house of the Lord forever."

It had been a long grueling day at the salon. My back hurt, my feet ached, my hands and fingers were sore and all I wanted to do was to get home, get something to eat, put my feet up and binge watch something, anything on TV. I couldn't get my work station cleaned up fast enough.

My last client of the day had been 30 minutes late and she begged me to please stay and do her hair: I stayed! She gave me a pretty decent tip for doing so, but my body was paying for it. I prayed "Lord, just help me to finish this one last client today. I thank you in advance; Amen." And boy O' boy, did he do it! I felt strength come to my body and my mind geared up for one more conversation. We talked about the latest happenings in the news, her family and job, the weather and just a little bit of entertainment gossip; (the harmless kind). Before I knew it, I was done. She thanked me, paid me and said, "See ya in two, (two weeks) peace!" I pocketed my tip and quickly began the clean-up.

I grabbed my purse and coat and began walking toward the door. It was now dark already; 6 pm on a Tuesday, October 23, windy and chilly evening. There was a cold breeze that blew and chilled my nose as I walked to my car about fifty feet away. All I could think about was food and putting my feet up. A smile crossed my face in anticipation: I couldn't wait! Just at that moment I heard something. It sounded like rustling leaves only heavier. I turned to look and see what it might be, but I didn't see anything, not even leaves. "Hmmmm!" I thought, "That's odd," As I didn't break stride, but kept walking, then, I heard it again.

"What in the world is that?", I said out loud to myself. Yet again, when I looked, nothing and no one was there that I could see.

Now at my car, I hit the button to unlock the doors and hurriedly jumped in and locked the doors. I looked around again now in the safety of my car, but saw nothing. I started the engine and my cell phone began to ring just as I put the gear in reverse. I put the gear back in park mode and took the call. "Hello!" "Hey sis, this is Annette, are you coming?" "Coming where" I said. To the church to help put together care packages for the homeless. Remember? Tonight we were all supposed to meet and put care packages together!" "Awwwww sis! I'd forgotten. And I'm exhausted. I've had such a hard day in the shop. Mrs. Williams complained about her perm. Janet said I cut too much of her hair for a trim. Yet she really needed at least another quarter inch taken. I left Betty under the dryer too long with color on her head, (laughing out loud). She looked like Mr. Heat Miser from that old Christmas cartoon, Rudolph the Red-Nosed Reindeer. I spent another thirty minutes toning and deep conditioning her afterwards. And to top it all off, Shirley was thirty minutes late! My body aches and I'm hungry!" "Awww but sis," Annette said, "You have to; it won't be the same without you. I'll buy you dinner if you come and you can sit the whole time while putting the care packages together. Deal?" Deal! I said and hung up. I put the car in drive mode and began driving to the church. Good thing it's only a couple of blocks from the salon. I don't know if I could have made it if it were any further.

When I pulled up to the church, I was able to pull right into an empty spot right in front. I was so happy I didn't have to park in the side lot and walk all the way around back to the front entrance. I slid the gear in Park, grabbed my purse and got out. I pushed the key fob to lock the doors and just as I did, I heard that rustling again. I looked around, yet again, nothing! I thought to myself, "Self, you're tired and you're hearing things; get it together!" I ran up the few steps to the front double doors, opened one and hurried in. I immediately saw Annette and went to give her a hug. Only I was intercepted by Mrs. Gladys Payne. Mrs. Payne is an 80 year old elder of the church who has seen and knows a lot of things. She doesn't take no mess from young folks, but one thing Mrs. Payne could do is pray, and get a prayer through to God: Powerful! "Mother Payne," as everyone affectionately calls her, "How are you?" I asked. "Sister Wright, when are you going to have those flyers for the upcoming Winter Fling completed? She asked in a stern voice, completely ignoring my greeting. You know it's only a couple of months away and we needed those flyers like, yesterday!" "Mother Payne, the printers promised me last week that they would be done today.

However, I just got off work and I came right over here, so I haven't had a chance to go by there and check on them. I will call them as soon as I find a place to park my tired feet. They don't close until eight." "Mmmm hum, you'd better," she said. "I love you Mother Payne!" I shouted as I walked off toward Annette and grabbed my seat. Annette gave me a huge apologetic hug and we both broke into laughter. "How ya doing girl?" Annette asked. "I'm EXHAUSTED!" But I'm here. "Well, slow down, take a few deep breaths and I'll be right back with some hot tea" she said. "Ooo, that sounds good." I kicked off my shoes and put my feet up in an empty chair directly in front of me.

Everything to make the care packages was already on the table and ready to go. A few had been made, so I followed the example of the completed packages and moved right along. When Annette came back with the tea, I was well on my fourth or fifth package. It smelled heavenly and tasted even more so. The warmth of the tea hit the spot and did wonders to take the chill off from the night air. After Annette sat down I began to tell her of the strange

occurrences that happened on the way to the church. "Wow!" She said. "You didn't see anyone around?" "No" I said; "Not a soul." It was kind of creepy. Now that I think about it, I think I am just overly tired and hungry from such a long and trying day at work.

When I get home and get a shower and get in my bed, I will be just fine. Nothing that a hot shower and a good nights sleep won't fix. "Yeah, you're probably right", Annette said. The hour and a half went by quickly. Annette is such a good friend and when we get together, the time flies. Mother Payne was busy with other church duties so I didn't see her anymore during the evening and that was just fine by me. Plus, I'd forgotten to call the printers and I didn't want to have to explain to her why. So I was glad she was busy. Along with the other twenty-five or so volunteers, we made a couple hundred care packages which everyone agreed was a huge success. We said a group prayer, gave our hugs to each other and I was on my way home, finally!

I found a parking spot right in front of my second floor apartment. I thought to myself, Wow! Another great parking spot, Favor is on my side. I could see the little night light through the curtains as I pulled up. I got out of my car, locked the door and that's when I heard it again. Only this time it sounded like footsteps right behind me. didn't see anyone when I pulled into the parking lot, so where could they have come from. I didn't even stop to turn around and look. I bolted up the stairs as fast as I could praying "Lord, my shield and my protector. Keep me safe and let there be nobody there." When I got to my door I had to fumble in my purse for my keys. "You idiot! Why didn't you get your keys out before you exited the car?" Ooo, my heart was racing and I was terrified as I now thought I heard footsteps coming up the stairs. "Help me Jesus! Help me Jesus! Help me Jesus!" I said. Finally I found them, unlocked the door and flew in, hopefully locking out whatever I thought I heard out there. "Thank you Jesus!" was all I could muster up as I put the dead bolt on the door.

I listened for just a few seconds to see if I heard anyone outside my door: Nothing! I kicked off my shoes at the door and dropped my purse in the first chair I saw as I made my way to the bathroom. Not only was I in a hurry to get a shower, but I also needed to use the toilet. All of the excitement made me have to

go after drinking all that tea. After relieving myself of excitement and tea I quickly jumped in the hot shower. The water was **w o n d e r f u l.** If this shower had a place to sit, I'd most assuredly would have sat down, but the warmth of the water almost made me forget how much my feet hurt. They felt better almost instantly and my tired achey muscles began to relax.

Soon however, my stomach let me know that it needed attention: I was hungry. Annette got me tea, but did not get me dinner. Truth be told, once we started talking and laughing, I forgot all about being hungry. Now though, was a different story. I needed sustenance like right now. I hopped out of the shower, dried off and put on my favorite cuddly pj's. They were warm and fuzzy and just what a cold fall night like tonight needed. I looked in the fridge to see what was in there that I could pop into the microwave and warm up. Hmmmm! Left over baked chicken from last night, 2-day old pizza or I could make a healthy salad with the lettuce, tomato and cucumber I had in the crisper. I decided to make a salad because I needed to use the veggies before they went bad. I also decided to shred a piece of chicken breast on top just to give it an extra boost of protein and flavor.

As I gathered my dinner and my drink, I went to sit in the living room and watch some TV. By this time the local nightly news was on and I was too tired to even flip through channels. I ate my salad and gazed mindlessly at the TV screen. I must have zoned out because a knock at the door jolted me back to reality. "Who could that be," I thought. I got up to take a look out the peep hole, but no one was there that I could see. I went to the large window of my living room to get a better view, but again, I didn't see anyone. I turned to go back to the couch and I heard the knock at the door again. "Okay, whoever's out there this is not funny I said. I'm calling the police right now. Go away!" I'm terrified, but I didn't let whoever is playing games on the other side of my door know that with my voice. I tried to sound as mad and as hard as I could under the circumstances. Inside however I was shaking in my house shoes. "Go away. I've already called the police and they are on their way." I hadn't of course, but they didn't know that. I was hoping it was just kids carrying on Halloween shenanigans a week before it's time and that the threat of the police being called would scare them away. "I hate Halloween, I said to myself. My mother stopped us from trick or

treating when we were little and reports on the news said kids were getting injured from razor blades in fruit and candy laced with drugs. That was all she needed to hear and we were never allowed to celebrate that holiday again. People are evil and crazy she said. "Who would want to hurt kids in this way?" Well, she wasn't giving them a chance to hurt her kids and she put a stop to the whole thing. As I thought about this I noticed a few minutes had passed and no more knocks came on the door.

I looked out the peep hole and I didn't see anyone so I assumed they got scared and ran off. I decided I'd had enough excitement for the day and I was going to bed. I switched off the TV and headed straight to my room.

Aww Man! It felt so good to fall into bed and snuggle under my weighted blanket and between those crisp sheets. When my head hit the pillow I thanked the Lord for another blessed and productive day and before I could say Amen, I was off in dreamland.

Running, running, running as fast as I could through a thick wooded area, but I didn't seem to be covering much ground. I'm exhausted, but it looks like I've only gone maybe five feet. Why do I feel so heavy? Why am I running so slow and a better question is, WHY AM I RUNNING? I soon found out. The footsteps got louder and louder behind me as I tried to run faster and faster, but seemed to get nowhere. I thought to myself, If I could fly, I'd gain more ground, get away faster. Before I knew it, I was in the air dodging tree limbs as I climbed above the trees.

Whoo hoo! I shouted as I now seemed to fly with no limits, no heaviness or boundaries. Surely I have left whatever it was following me way behind. I laughed with excitement as I tested my newfound skill. I ascended up into the clouds, I dove down like a seagull diving for a meal only to level out right before hitting the ground; it was exhilarating and I felt invincible. In the air however, especially since I was moving so fast, I couldn't hear the danger behind me. I was only alerted as I flew over water with the moon shining brightly over the water I caught a glimpse of a light. A quick flash from off the water, when I looked behind me there they were. They were huge winged warrior like angelic creatures following me. They were at least double, maybe even triple my size. How do I know that I asked myself; it was just sort of instinctive; I just knew. What do I do? I was frightened and I couldn't out fly them; they were gaining on me and yet toying with me; hanging back just a little on purpose.

Girl you've brought the weird events of your day into your dreams. Why? What are you doing, I thought to myself. Do I keep flying? Do I land and confront them? Do I force myself to wake-up? What? I was frantic with questions and not knowing what to do.

I woke up!

My heart was racing and I was sweating so much I had to wipe my forehead. I glanced at my alarm clock on my night stand; it read 2:00 am. What seemed like only half an hour in my dream had been four hours? Wow! As I scanned the room it was just as I left it when I went to sleep except as I looked over my left shoulder I saw them and jumped and screamed simultaneously. I hit the opposite wall with a hard thud, slid to the floor and covered my face with my blanket. No! No! No! No! No! I kept saying, hoping that when I opened my eyes they'd be gone. I slowly peeled back the covers from my head and I opened my eyes, but they were still there. Those huge warrior-like angelic looking beings were standing right next to my bed. Shoulder to shoulder they stood, tall in complete silence with their heads touching my ceiling. They took my breath away.

They were beautiful! There was a glow that radiated from them that seemed to illuminate the room. When flying in my dream looking back at them from that view and being so terrified, I couldn't see their beauty. But now, in the light that radiated from them piercing the darkness of my bedroom, at 2:00 o'clock in the morning they were absolutely beautiful. Their beauty calmed my rapid breathing. I began to settle down a little while yet still afraid if that's at all possible. My eyes followed up their semi-armored-like figures. I couldn't see their feet because my bed blocked that view, but about mid calf their muscular legs stood out to me. Wow! I mouthed. I then noticed their skirt wrapped around their waist which dropped just below their knees. The skirt had thin strips of steel like shields spaced around it. Around their torsos were full hammered iron breastplates. They were intricately etched and beautiful. Their arms were bare and looked as if they worked out in a gym ALL DAY! Their faces chiseled: square jaw lines, high cheek bones and gorgeous eyelashes that all men seem to be blessed with but don't appreciate. And their hair: dreadlocks? Really? Warrior angels with dreadlocks? I chuckled to myself just a bit.

By the time my eyes met theirs, my heart rate was beating almost normal. Their big brown compassionate eyes let me know they weren't a threat, as they never shifted from me. I seemed to be their primary focus. I finally got the courage to speak, now knowing they weren't here to kill me, I asked "Who are you and what do you want? Have you been following me around all day?" You scared me! What do you think you're doing?" I had a thousand questions and a lot to get off my chest since they weren't there to hurt me. One of them spoke and said, "we've been assigned to you by our Creator." "Assigned to me?" I repeated. "What does that mean? And who is your creator?" The other one spoke and said, "Our Creator goes by many names. To us He is Creator; maker of Heaven and earth and all that is within, The Most High God, The Great I AM, that I AM." I said, "You mean GOD?" "Yes!" They said in unison. "God assigned you to me?" "I have my very own angels assigned to me?" Wow! I said as I shook my head looking at the floor between my knees. Wow! I can't believe this. "Why?" I asked. One of them spoke again and said, "When you were born God assigned angels to watch over you. You are precious to Him. He formed you and knew you even in your mother's womb. When you gave your life to Jesus this past summer, you accepted Him as your Savior. You asked Him to come into your heart. You asked the Holy Spirit to come and teach you all that you needed to know to help you in your new life. As soon as you said yes to Jesus' invitation to eternal life, we were dispatched to bring answers to your prayers and to fight off the enemy on your behalf when he tries to attack you. You have been with me since that day?" The other spoke and said, "We have been with you since the very moment of your Yes." "Why now? Why am I just realizing that you've been with me?" The other spoke and said, "because your heart is tender toward God. Our Creator sees that your heart wants to please Him. You want what He wants. He is pleased with your prayers and He loves the sound of your voice. He loves visiting you in your dreams and showing you many things about Himself and yourself. He appreciates you spending time reading and studying His word. He loves you so much. Not just because you do these things, but because that's Who He is: Love; and nothing can separate you from His love." The other angel then spoke and said, "Our Creator opened your eyes and let you see us as a gift to increase your security, confidence and faith, and for His good pleasure. We will not be visible to you all the time, but just know that we will always

be with you as He is always with you, just as He promised. He will never leave you nor forsake you.

By this time, I am totally relaxed. All fear has dissipated, although I still can't stand up. I tried, but their presence was heavy. So there, sitting in that glow, a million more questions come to mind, but one of them speaks and says, "We must go now, but only for what on earth will feel like a millisecond: our Creator is beckoning us. However, just know that we will be back before you miss us and the Holy Spirit is always with you." With that, just before they disappeared I asked them, "Do you have names? What are your names?" The one said, "I'm Goodness and I'm Mercy" the other said, and then they were gone.

Psalm 23

1. The Lord is my Shepherd, I shall not want.
2. He makes me to lie down in green pastures: he leaders me besides the still waters.
3. He restores my soul: He leads me in the paths of righteousness for His name's sake.
4. Yea, though I walk through the valley of the shadow of death, I will fear no evil: for thou are with me; they rod and thy staff they comfort me.
5. Thou prepares a table before me in the presence of my enemies: thou anoint my head with oil; my cup runneth over.
6. Surely goodness and mercy shall follow me all the days of my life: and I will dwell in the house of the LORD for ever.
Amen

After reading Psalms 23 and meditating on it, write down your thoughts of these promises from God. Is there a verse that sticks out the most to you and why?

_____
_____
_____
_____
_____
_____
_____
_____
_____
_____
_____
_____
_____
_____
_____
_____
_____
_____
_____
_____

The Lord is my light and my salvation; whom shall I fear? The Lord is the strength of my life; of whom shall I be afraid? Psalm 127:1 KJV

Did you know that you have angels assigned to you? Don't let them be idle, they await your prayers to put them to work and bring answers from the LORD.

The LORD God is my strength, ... Habakkuk 3:19 KJV

The Book of Amos a poem

The LORD roars from Zion and thunders from Jerusalem
The lion has roared, who will not fear?
The Sovereign LORD has spoken-who can but prophesy?
The LORD of heaven, He draws us near.

The God of judgement: The Sovereign LORD
The God of Justice: Let it roll like a river: righteousness a never-ending stream.
So our God, as He is today. An awesome God of glory beams.

The God of Truth, our shield and buckler,
The God who cares for the least of these:
the poor
the oppressed
the widows
and fatherless,
the orphans and strangers
You have respect for all of them please

The Lord God Almighty, El Shaddai
The God who laments after His children with pleas'
The God who calls out, for our repentance
Another chance He continues to give
Another chance to repent on our knees

Do two walk together unless they agree?
He's the God who reveals His thoughts to men
Seek me and live the Sovereign LORD says
Hate evil, love good, maintain justice
I'll be your God, you'll be my people
Of which my love will never end

The God of reason: Come, let us reason together
The God of compassion
Who only wants our hearts
Not our traditions, nor religiosity

The God who forgives
And gives us a brand new start
The God who swears by Himself alone: His Holiness

The pride of Jacob, He'll forever be
Inspite of all His goodness and all His blessings
He sadly says, Yet you've not returned to me!

The God with no beginning
The God with no end
In His ever-loving mercy and compassion he'll be
The God of restoration, restores us again
To Great harvests and full barns
quivers of children, blessings untold we'll see

For eyes have not seen, nor ears have heard,
All that's in store for us from Jesus Christ our King
He's gone to prepare, a place in heaven
for each of His children, for eternity

The days are coming, declares the LORD
The days are coming, new wine from mountains will flow
The four corners of the earth, will give up my children
My Word have I spoken, and **it will be so!**

Seek good, and not evil, ... Hate the evil and love the good, ...
Amos 5:14 &15 KJV

Can two walk together, except they be agreed? Amos 3:3 KJV

Who Does Christ Say I AM!

If you study the book of Ephesians, especially chapters 1 and 2, you will see many names of which the LORD calls you. To be totally transparent, I struggled with this for a long time. Low self-esteem, low self-worth and rejection kept me from seeing me as my Lord and Savior saw me. Getting some deliverance has helped me to accept the things the Lord says I am because I believe His word. Yet, sometimes when I'm in a crowd of people or I've not properly armored myself with the word and promises of God for the day as I should, the enemy tries to tell me that I'm inadequate, not good enough and that I am *'the very least'* of these, and I have to remind myself of what the Lord says.

I love to watch movies. Oftentimes because I see a lot of things prophetically, I watch with a different eye and the Holy Spirit will give me a word of encouragement or exhortation or comfort for myself or someone else. And having raised two children of my own and now raising another generation, I've watched my share of Disney cartoons and movies. One of my kid's favorites coming up was The Lion King. I've seen both the original and the 2019 remake. There is a scene in the movie where Simba has to be reminded of who he is. Rafiki has Simba to take a look at his reflection in a pool of water and he asks Simba, *"Do you see?* **He lives inside of you."** In *t*he next scene the spirit of Mufasa as seen in a cloud appears and Mufasa says to his son, **"Remember who you are! You are a king!** As the cloud of Mufasa begins to disappear, Simba says, **"Dad, don't leave me!"** Of which Mufasa responds, **"I've never left you and I never will."**

The Holy Spirit used this movie one day, after my twentieth time watching it probably, and clear as a beautiful sun shiny day something pierced every fiber of my being and I began to weep. It was nothing but God! It was suddenly and unexpected! **I got it!, I got it!** I am not who the opinion of man says that I am! (not mother, not father, sister nor brother)
I am not who the world says that I am! (not teacher, not boss, government nor society)
I am not who I may even think or say that I am! (low, the least, nothing, just a woman)

But I am who God my heavenly father says that I am! I must align my thinking with His heart and mind for me. I must come into agreement with who He says that I am! And this is what He says.

I am:

Faithful	Ephesians 1:1
Blessed	Ephesians 1:3
Chosen	Ephesians 1:4
Holy	
Without Blame	
Adopted	Ephesians 1:5
Accepted	Ephesians 1:6
Redeemed	Ephesians 1:7
Forgiven	Ephesians 1:7
Wise	Ephesians 1:8
Prudent	Ephesians 1:8
Made aware of the mystery of His good will	Ephesians 1:9
Inheritor	Ephesians 1:11
Saved	Ephesians 1:13
Sealed	Ephesians 1:13
Revelation	Ephesians 1:17
Enlightened	Ephesians 1:18
Understanding	Ephesians 1:18
Called	Ephesians 1:18
Quickened	Ephesians 2:1
Loved	Ephesians 2:4
Seated with Jesus in heavenly places	Ephesians 2:6
Raised up with Jesus	Ephesians 2:6
A workmanship of God	Ephesians 2:10
Ordained	Ephesians 2:10
Made High	Ephesians 2:13
Reconciled	Ephesians 2:16
A Fellow Citizens with the Saints of the Household of God	Ephesians 2:19
A Holy Temple in the Lord	Ephesians 2:21
A Habitation of God through the Spirit	Ephesians 2:22
Bold	Ephesians 3:12
Confident	Ephesians 3:12
Beloved	Song of Solomon 5:1
Beautiful	Song of Solomon 6:4

At the same time, God also gave us gifts in the names as well.

God gave:

Holiness	Ephesians 1:4
Inheritance	Ephesians 1:11
Redemption	Ephesians 1:7
Wisdom	Ephesians 1:8
Prudence	Ephesians 1:8
Purpose	Ephesians 1:11
Hope	Ephesians 1:18
Salvation	Ephesians 1:13
Holy Spirit	Ephesians 2:18 & 22
Covenant	Ephesians 2:12
Spirit of wisdom, Revelation and knowledge	Ephesians 1:17
Enlightened understanding	Ephesians 1:18
A calling	Ephesians 1:18
Power	Ephesians 1:18
New Life	Ephesians 2:15
Mercy	Ephesians 2:4
Love	Ephesians 2:4
A seat in heavenly places	Ephesians 2:6
kindness	Ephesians 2:7
Grace	Ephesians 2:5
Peace	Ephesians 2:14
Access to himself	Ephesians 2:18

No longer do I let the devil try to compare me to others.
By the grace of God I am who I am (1Corinthians 1:4);
I am fearfully and wonderfully made (Psalm 139:14)
In His image (Genesis 1:26) and
My beloved is mine and I am His. (Song of Solomon 2:16)
Nothing can separate me from His love (Romans 8:38-39) and
No one can snatch me from out of his hand.
I'm learning to walk in the full, all encompassing love, authority and power of Christ.

Father I stretch my hands to thee. Please forgive me for not seeing and believing Your word and who You say that I am. Forgive me Father for believing the lie of the devil; I repent Lord.

Thank you Father through the Holy Spirit for showing me who I truly am: a child of The Most High God, loved, saved, redeemed who has a place at the throne of grace and mercy. Thank you Father for opening my eyes to Your Truth and Your love. In Jesus name Amen.

And God said unto Moses, I AM THAT I AM: and He said, Thus shalt thou say unto the children of Israel, I AM hath sent me unto you.
Exodus 3:14 KJV

Who do you _KNOW_ that you are? Who are you? Write it and declare it! Speak it here every day until you truly believe it and it becomes a part of you to your core.

But by the grace of God I am what I am: ... 1 Corinthians 15:10 KJV

LOVE IS

This is something the Lord God gave me one Sunday morning as I was deep in prayer with a few of my intercessor sisters. He let me peek inside of His heart at that moment and what I saw was so beautiful, so compassionate, so loving and so full, complete and all encompassing. I wept like a baby. I'm sure that I experienced only a tiny portion of the true love that God has for us. I believe we'll never really know, because of our humanity, the depth, height, width, length and breadth of His love until we get to heaven. But on that day He let me see and feel His heart and I am forever grateful for the encounter; it was overwhelming and this is the word that came out of that experience.

Love is the fuel
Love is the fire
Love is the reason God does what He does and we do what we do
Love is why we pray
Love is why we lay hands to heal and deliver
Love is why we prophesy
Love is why we decree and speak and declare
Love is why God delays his judgement upon the earth; for it is not His will that any should perish, but that all may come into the knowledge of Jesus Christ and be saved
Love is what drives us
Love is what drives Him:
Jesus had compassion on the sick, the infirmed, the deformed, diseased, bewitched and tormented. HE healed them all.
Love is what fed the 5000 and then the 4000 and what feeds us now
Love corrects
Love restores
Love covers a multitude of sins 1Peter 4:8
Love is our portion, the children's bread and though the world doesn't know it or refuses to accept it, His Love is what they are searching for.

For God so loved the world that He gave His only begotten son, that whosoever believeth in Him should not perish, but have everlasting life.
John 3:16 KJV
God Loves the sinner, yet hates the sin.
God Loves the backslider; for He's married to them. There is no breaking of covenant by Him.

God Loves the Protestant, the Jewish, the Baptist, the Catholic, the Evangelical, the Lutheran, the Pentecostal, the Buddhist, the Jehovah's Witness, even the Satanist and all other man-made religious divisions; He wants us **ALL** saved: to accept the free salvation bought by His son Jesus Christ and His shed blood.
God Loves the black, the white, the yellow, the brown, the policemen, the judges, the lawyers, the priest, the laymen, the widows, the orphaned, the housewives, the imprisoned, the thieves: He redeemed one while yet hanging on the cross.
God Loves the brokenhearted, the rejected, the dejected, the lost, the confused, those who don't know who they are:

HE LOVES!
Nothing can separate us from His Love Romans 8:39
Love suffers long and is kind, love envies not, love boasts not, is not puffed up, Love does not behave unseemly, seeks not her own, is not easily provoked, thinks no evil; rejoices not in iniquity, but rejoices in truth; bears all things, believes all things, hopes in all things, endures all things.

Love never fails! 1 Corinthians 13:4-8 KJV

I say all this to say, as the LORD let me peek into His heart, He is pouring out; He has poured out His Love upon the world and we shall see the manifestation of His Love upon the earth and ALL it's glory; things we've never seen before with mass healings, mass miracles, mass deliverances, signs and wonders done through those who are yielded, willing and obedient. His glory will fill the temples of each yielded believer and
we shall see it!,

we shall see it!

we shall see it!

Be still and know that, I AM GOD! - All will be silent before Him.
His Love, the driving force
His heart melts for us
His heart calls out to us, for us
His heart is **poured out!**,
                         is poured out!
                                             is poured out!

Upon the earth, Do you not see it? Do you not know it? Can you not perceive it?
I AM here!
                 I AM here NOW!
                                 Receive me!
Know me!
        Learn of me!
        Love me as I have Loved You!

God is speaking! He is always speaking!
Let them who have ears to hear, hear what the Spirit of the LORD is saying Amen.

God is Love. 1 John 4:8 KJV

Be not overcome of evil, but overcome evil with good.

Romans 12:21 KJV

Thou Prepares a Table

Come with me for just a minute. Let your imagination loose and imagine a table. A very long table that runs as far as the eye can see. A table with no end. This table is beautifully set with fine pearl china; the choicest of high gloss silverware and the most translucent of crystal stemware the likes of which have never been seen before. Each place setting is perfect and prepared with care. Running down the middle of the table are clear vases of stunning fresh flowers of every kind, every color, shape, size and fragrance. The colors are vibrant, the fragrance is pure, sweet and amazing. You soon notice the savory smells of the meals that are being placed in front of each person seated at the table. Each meal looks so appetizing: prepared to perfection according to your taste. Anything and everything you can imagine because the Host of this feast has spared no expense. He is not limited by money. He has gone to great lengths to ensure your enjoyment and pleasure.

Now that your senses have been awakened, your next thought might be, but why? Who is this feast for? Who set all this up? And where is this table?
The who: for You!
The who from: The Most High God of Heaven and Earth!
The why: Because our God, the Great I AM, THAT I AM, that Great Shepherd of the Sheep is just good like that; He loves to lavish on His children. Secondly, because He knows you're tired and weary and in need of refreshing and rest. The great God of rest and refreshing has prepared a table for you, with you in mind, down to the detail. Our Father in heaven painstakingly planned and laid out the table and feast.

And you won't dine alone. There will be other brothers and sisters in Christ, like-minded, Kingdom-advancing brethren dining with you. Great food! Great conversation! Great atmosphere.

Getting renewed in the spirit of your mind (Ephesians 4:23). And the service is awesome! Yet there is something familiar about the service that you can't quite put your finger on. Those serving seem happy. They have a smile on their faces and within their hearts that seem to leap from them.

They are attentive and punctual to all they are serving with no lack in their service. It's done with anticipation and excitement. They seemed to move to a song within them, a worship between them and the Lord. An internal synchronization that gives them life, energy and an unexplainable joy.

As they served, it finally occurs to you where you know some of your brethren from: ministry! These were brothers and sisters in Christ that you had the privilege of serving with at one time or another. The brother you served with at the Bronx soup kitchen; the missions trip to Africa to build schools and dig wells; the homeless shelter in Los Angeles where you passed out blankets and prayed with despondent individuals and families and the pastors' conference in many cities attended across the U.S.

Having come to this realization, you ask one of the servers,
"Do I know you? Didn't we do missions together a while back?"
The server looks at you and with a big smile says,
'Yes, in South America some while back. I have to tell ya, that was the hardest, yet most rewarding thing I've ever done next to this" he says. So I ask him,
"Where is this place? How did we get here?"
The server began to tell me his story.
"After many years of traveling, missions and pastoring, I grew weary and disenchanted. My body was exhausted and my mind tired of thankless people and my emotions were a mess. I knew I needed rest. My spirit was drained. One day in desperation and exhaustion, I called out to God, "Father I need you!" My soul is weary, my body is tired, my mind is frazzled: something has to give."
In that very moment He answered.
One moment I'm in my church study on my knees crying out and the next, I'm here. Like the Apostle Paul said, whether in the body or out of the body, I cannot tell: God knows, 2 Corinthians 12:3.
But I really didn't care: I'm here and I feel awesome.
Then I heard a voice say, "Sit and eat." So I found an empty chair and sat down. Immediately food was brought to me.

They seemed to just 'know' exactly what I liked and wanted. I gave thanks to God the Father and dug right in.

Man, I'm telling you, I've never tasted my food before until now. My tastes buds exploded. I ate until I was good and full. As I received my refreshing from the food for my physical body, I began to get refreshed in my soul. I listened and joined in on various conversations going on around me. I smiled, I sighed, I laughed and I wept while listening to the different experiences my fellow brothers and sisters had serving and advancing the Kingdom. I tell ya, as I listened and shared, all of the weariness and loneliness of ministry began to lift off me. It simply evaporated. I felt a renewed energy and hope ignite within me. I Didn't want to move from my spot. The community that I felt, and the peace and comfort released… I just wanted to sit there forever.

However, there was a small tug in my spirit to get up and serve. It was now my turn to serve in this capacity and now, I do it with gladness. I don't know how long I have here before I'm back 'there', home again, so I want to take advantage of this and enjoy each and every second of His presence right here.

Periodically I'd noticed a brother or sister would get up, grab an apron and begin to serve. New wearied souls would sit down and take their place. This went on time and time again. After I'd eaten and shared and communed, that tug in my spirit got a little stronger and I knew it was time for me to serve and you will know as well. So just as the Father said, Sit! Eat! Find rest for your weary soul and when it's time for you to serve, you will know and you too will do it with gladness of heart." After he said that, he was gone and I sat and enjoyed the Father's meal, His service and His presence at His table; the table prepared just for me, for us.

Matthew 11:28 KJV Come unto me all ye that labour and are heavy laden, and I will give you rest.

The Twenty Third Psalm - KJV

1. The Lord is my shepherd; I shall not want.
2. He maketh me to lie down in green pastures: He leadeth me beside the still waters.
3. He restoreth my soul: He leadeth me in paths of righteousness for His name's sake.
4. Yea, though I walk through the valley of the shadow of death, I will fear no evil: for Thou art with me; Thy rod and Thy staff they comfort me.
5. Thou preparest a table before me in the presence of mine enemies: Thou anoints my head with oil; my cup runneth over.
6. Surely goodness and mercy shall follow me all the days of my life; and I will dwell in the house of the Lord for ever.

Trust in the Lord with all thine heart and lean not unto your own understanding. In all thy ways acknowledge Him, and He shall direct thy paths. Proverbs 3:5-6 KJV

O taste and see that the Lord is good: ... Psalm 34:8 KJV

Prayer

On one of my many walks; talking to myself and talking to God, the question arose within me "What is prayer anyway?"
Merriam-Webster says prayer is a petition to God or a god.
Prayer is simply talking to God
Prayer is listening for His voice, whether it be audible, an imprint or impression on my heart, hearing His voice within my spirit or my inner man, through a dream or a vision, a knowing, a gut feeling, a sign on a billboard,
Communicating!
Me talking to Him,
Him talking to me, which means I have to stop talking and listen for His response.

They say that the audible voice of God is rare. I have to agree.
I've only heard the audible voice of God twice in my life; once as a teenager and once as an adult. When I was a teenager maybe 15 or 16 years old, I was in my bedroom. I don't remember exactly what I was doing, but it was evening, after dinner and everyone in the house was just chilling. Out of nowhere I hear my name
"Madeline!"
I stop what I'm doing and I look around. I then hear it again,
"Madeline!"
I go to the room next to mine where my father was relaxing watching television after dinner. I ask him
"Did you call me?"
He says "No"
I go back to my room and I begin to ponder; "Who called me?" "Where did that voice come from?"
I then begin to think maybe it was God. But I don't inquire or press it any further. I just go on with what I was doing, thinking maybe I will hear the voice a third time, but it never came.

I heard the voice of God again as an adult. I was now married with two small children. It was a day I had decided to fast and pray, committing the day to the Lord. I'm at work in the records department of the hospital, filing and pulling records as requests come in and I'm praying as I'm working. I say to the Lord in prayer, "You know I love you Lord" and almost immediately the

Lord responds audibly, "Do you?" I stopped dead in my tracks, arms full of files and records and I look around to see who said that. I go over to the next isle of records and one of my coworkers is by herself filing records. I look to the front of the office and another coworker is at the computer silently working. Hmmmm! Neither of them said anything to me, and besides, the voice that just spoke to me sounded like a man's voice. "God, was that you?" I was shook. I stopped praying. I didn't know what else to say. God himself has just spoke to me and questioned my love for Him; what was I to say? That brief prayer ROCKED MY WHOLE LIFE; IT CHANGED MY WHOLE WORLD.

It took me a very long time for me to profess my love to the Lord again. I dared not say it until I knew in my heart there was no question from me or God about my love for Him. I wouldn't say it, I wouldn't sing a song with that phrase in it and it made me very aware and cautious of what I said to God. If I didn't mean it, I didn't say it. If I was not sure about it, I didn't say it. If the words of a song said something that I knew I wasn't doing, I wasn't singing it! Case in point. The song by Tasha Cobb-Leonard, For Your Glory, there is a line in that song that says "For your glory, I'll do anything, just to see you, to behold you as my king."
Well, I would not sing that song because I knew in my heart of hearts I wasn't doing anything and everything within my power to see Him, and behold Him. This song speaks of crossing the hottest deserts, and traveling near or far and I didn't feel I was doing everything I could, should or would and I was determined not to hear His audible voice again questioning my love or dedication to Him. I didn't want to hear "Are you?"
I wasn't going to sing a lie.

In the book of Numbers 6, God says "And thou shalt love the Lord thy God with all thine heart, with all thy soul and with all thy might". In Mark 12:30 KJV it goes even a little further, "And thou shalt love the Lord thy God with all thy heart, and with all thy soul, and with all thy mind and with all thy strength."

Now I know that the Holy Spirit doesn't condemn, but He will convict. The devil condemns and he condemned me through the religious spirit I had within me. Trying to perform my way into the Kingdom. Keep trying! If I pray enough, fast enough, read

enough; earn my way into God's good graces, then He'll accept me, love me and not question my love for Him.
It's never enough! I would feel bad about myself and get on myself for not doing more.
I had to rid myself of religion and the condemnation.
I had to stop trying to perform to be accepted and just receive, because every good and perfect gift from God is free; there should be no striving for it and His blessings make us rich and adds no sorrow, Proverbs 10:22.
"How do I do this? I don't know how?
Lord help me," I cried out.
Talking to the author and finisher of my faith; my Abba Father
The writer of my book, that He penned, which exists in heaven to be lived out here on earth.
You are my first! The first called; the first looked to; the first relied upon; the first in mind and thought at the start of my day; my last thought before drifting to sleep; and my everything in between.
Your word says that we should pray without ceasing 1 Thes. 5:17 and that we should look to you morning, noon and night Psalm 55:17.

And Yet

I am desperate to hear from you; to hear your voice. Your children, and even this world of sinners, unaware, are desperate to hear a word from you.
One Word!
Desperate to hear your sweet voice
Desperate for your instruction
Desperate for your revelation
Desperate for your wisdom
Desperate to hear Your plan for my life
Desperate! Desperate! Desperate! For just one word from you Lord can change the whole outcome of our lives.
Desperate for your still small voice
Desperate for your thunderous voice
Desperate for the sound in the wind that carries your whisper
Desperate for you Lord in any way, shape, form or fashion

Desperate:
    a. involving or employing extreme measures in an attempt to escape defeat or frustration
    b. suffering extreme need
    c. of extreme intensity
    d. shocking, outrageous

Desperate, yet not in despair
Never at a loss of hope because we hope in Jesus. His name is Jesus. Knowing that he hears us and will answer us because He is true to His word and cannot lie. He delivers us out of all of our troubles if we'll just call on His great name.
Like blind Bartemaeous, who called out to Jesus when he heard Jesus was coming. The people in the crowd told him to keep quiet! Shut up! But Bartemaeous called out even the more. He was desperate for a word, a touch, a healing from Savior; the Only One who could help.
Desperation got this man his eyesight back
Desperation got the attention of Jesus Christ
Desperate!
It's all in how you see it; It's all in what you need and what you'll do to get it.

It's risky!
The centurion soldier was desperate for his servant and took a risk
The Jewish priest was desperate for his daughter and took a risk
The ten lepers were desperate for themselves and each other and they took a risk. One was even more so; he was grateful as well and he became whole.
The Canaanite mother requesting the children's bread was desperate and took the risk for her possessed daughter.
The "Help my unbelief" father was desperate for his demoniac son, he took the risk and his son was set free.
The woman with the bloody issue of twelve years was desperate having spent all she had on doctors who did not deliver. Believing she pressed her unclean self through that crowd, bowed down and touched the hem of His garment and IMMEDIATELY her issue stopped.
Friends tearing off a roof where Jesus taught, just to lower their crippled friend to the feet of Jesus: desperate.

Peter stepping off the boat into the water: desperate.

Even Jesus prayed, talked to His Father. There were many times He went off to find a place to be alone and pray. He too wanting to talk and hear the voice of God.
Mark 14:33-36
And Jesus who took Peter, James and John to the garden with Him to pray "And He began to be deeply distressed and troubled. My soul is overwhelmed with sorrow to the point of death, Jesus said to them. Stay here and watch. And He went forward a little, and fell on the ground, and prayed that, if it were possible, the hour might pass from him. And He said Abba, Father, all things are possible unto thee; take away this cup from me; nevertheless not my will, but what thou wilt."
Jesus; desperate!

But He knew He had a job to do and His love saw it through unto the end. But there was a moment, when His full humanity kicked in and He wanted the hour to be over, He wanted the assignment to be lifted, He wanted the cup to pass from Him; but God!
God His Father gave Him strength
God His Father gave Him peace
God His Father gave Him what His physical human self needed for the hour because His time had come.
Prayer
Simply talking to God
Sharing your heart with His
Communicating
Communing; Spirit to spirit

Please pray!
Keep in touch with Him; daily
Stay desperate for Him and pursue Him with all you have.

Nor height, nor depth, nor any other creature, shall be able to separate us from the love of God, which is in Christ Jesus our Lord.
Romans 8:39 KJV

I am my beloved's and my beloved is mine… Song of Solomon 6:3 KJV

WISDOM AND UNDERSTANDING

Proverbs 4:7 KJV say, "Wisdom is the principal thing: therefore get wisdom: and in all thy getting get understanding."

Pondering this one day, after praying and asking the Lord for more wisdom to handle a certain situation, later that evening while reading a book called 101 Prophetic Ways God Speaks by Hakeem Collins; I came across the chapter entitled 'Wisdom Of God'. It talks about the difference between godly wisdom and earthly wisdom and how we must be discerning enough to know the difference. While reading through this chapter a light bulb went off in my spirit. What the Holy Spirit revealed to me in that moment was when we ask for godly wisdom which is **"knowledge which is perfect"** as Mr. Collins explains in his book, God gives to us liberally when we ask as it says in James 1:5. But when we ask for God's wisdom: perfect knowledge, we have to know how to apply it. This is where understanding comes into play. According to the Merriam Webster dictionary to Understand means "to grasp the meaning of; to have thorough technical acquaintance with or expertise; to accept as a fact or truth or regard as plausible without utter certainty. To understand according to the Strongs Concordance in Hebrew means "to separate mentally; distinguish; diligently direct; be prudent; wise/wisdom. Also, because the Hebrew language is a language of pictures, when the word understand is looked up it says, **"To see the name"** Here is an excellent explanation and example according to the book Hebrew Word Pictures by Dr. Frank T. Seekins, pages 220 and 192 respectively, and so I will let you read it straight from his book.

 **Obey:** The Hebrew word שָׁמַע shama means *hear, understand* and *obey*. The word picture describes how all of these function together. If I hear the name, I see the essence of something. If you tell a thirsty person to not drink the water in the glass and then leave the room, they will be tempted to take a drink anyway. But if you tell them that the glass is used to clean out the sewage so that they *see the name* or the real nature of the water in the glass, they now hear so that they understand and they will obey.

Because God is called *The Name* or הַשֵׁם *Ha-Shem* in Hebrew, this word picture carries a stronger meaning. Job argued with God, until in Job 42:5 he said, "*I have heard of You by the hearing of the ear, But now my eye sees You. Therefore ... I repent.*" When Job saw God (The Name) he understood, who God was, who he was, and changed.

The word faith is only used twice in the Old Testament (KJV), but the word שָׁמַע shama is used 1159 times. This is a foundational Jewish concept and is found in Romans 10:17 *So then faith comes by hearing, and hearing by the word of God.* Dwight Moody knew this truth when he put a sign on his pulpit to remind himself of the purpose of his preaching, it simply said "Sir, we would see Jesus".

Faith is not about my faithfulness, nor is it about my will power, it is about God's faithfulness, about our seeing, knowing and therefore trusting (and easily obeying) Him.

I mean isn't this why we're asking for His wisdom, so that we can apply it appropriately and be obedient? Understanding is the ability to apply. Understanding is the willingness to obey. To apply is action; it's movement; it's **faith forward obedience**. I really don't think that God would give you His perfect knowledge without also giving you the understanding of that knowledge to be able to apply it; move in faith in obedience. But it is always good that when you pray for wisdom, pray for the understanding as well. Pray for a heart to be obedient so that you can apply His perfect knowledge to your situation. The verses that also come to mind which I feel is connected to this is also found in James; it's James chapter 2 beginning at verse 14 through the end of the chapter. It speaks of faith ("So then faith comes by hearing and hearing by the word of God." Romans 10:17) and works and how your faith, in order for it to be true faith has to have some action behind it; obedience. How will someone know you have faith if you don't act it out? How will you know where your faith is if you don't move on it? So in my getting understanding of how godly wisdom works:

First, we must **hear** to have **faith to believe in Him** and that **He is!** And that He is a rewarder of those that diligently seek Him. Hebrews 11:6 We must hear His word.

Secondly, after hearing His word, believe enough to **ask Him** for His wisdom which He liberally gives to all men. James 1:5

Thirdly, when we receive God's wisdom, His perfect knowledge, ask for the **understanding** on how to apply His wisdom to your particular circumstance. Proverbs 4:7

Fourth, show your understanding of His wisdom by moving in faith: obedience, on what He has told you or showed you.

Proverbs 2:2 KJV "So that thou incline thine ear unto wisdom, and **apply** thine heart to understanding;"

This is how you know that you truly have an understanding of the wisdom God has given you; you put it into action: You move in obedience.
Faith without works is dead!
Wisdom without understanding/obedience will it avail much?
Knowledge without application impacts no one!
We must move!
It requires some action!
We must be obedient!

"Wisdom is the principal thing: (God's perfect knowledge) therefore get wisdom: and in all thy getting get understanding, (Obey)" Proverbs 4:7

Father God I thank You for Your word that says that if we lack wisdom, ask, and You will give unto all men liberally. I also ask and I thank You for the understanding of how to apply Your wisdom. Lord expand the capacity of my heart to receive more of Your infinite perfect knowledge and expand my capacity to always be willing and obedient to every word You speak to me whether it be through Your written word, through dreams and visions, an impression upon my heart, or dropped down into my spirit, however and whenever You choose to speak, let me show my understanding of Your wisdom through my obedience. In Jesus holy name, Amen.

Think of a time when you've prayed for more wisdom on how to handle a certain situation. When God gave you the wisdom or the answer, how did you apply it? How did it change you or your situation?

_____
_____
_____
_____
_____
_____
_____
_____
_____
_____
_____
_____
_____
_____
_____
_____
_____
_____

If any of you lack wisdom, let him ask of God, that giveth to all men liberally, and upbraideth not; and it shall be given him. James 1:5 KJV

To know **wisdom** and instruction; to perceive the words of understanding; Proverbs 1:2 KJV

ENDURE

While driving the Lord gave me a revelation on "'Enduring' until the end". Yeah, I've read and heard this word before, but today it was like an exclamation point and period was put on the end of that phase. Like in **Ecclesiastes 12:13** Solomon says, "Let us hear the <u>**conclusion of the whole matter:**</u> Fear God and keep His commandments: for this is the whole duty of man."

Matthew 24:13 and **Mark 13:3** both say, "But he that shall endure unto the end, the same shall be saved."

<u>**Endure**</u> in the New Strong's Exhaustive Concordance of the Bible; 5578 in the Greek is **Hupomeno** which means to stay under, behind, i.e., to remain, to undergo, i.e., trials, have fortitude, to persevere, to abide, to suffer, to be patient, to tarry behind.

For the Believers, those who believe in Jesus Christ and trust in Him, it's about enduring:

           Keep going!
         Don't give up!
       Push forward!
    One step at a time!
Never quit!

This is a race of sorts, but not a competition with your brothers and sisters in Christ, it's a self-paced race: just make it to the end.

Paul said in **Hebrews 12:1**, "Wherefore seeing we also are compassed about with so great a cloud of witnesses, let us lay aside very weight and sin which doth so easily beset us, and **let us run with patience the race** that is set before us."

You're not even trying to get a personal best; you're simply trying to make it to Heaven, the finish line! The presence of God is the goal! Seeing Jesus face-to-face and the TRUE, ALL encompassing Glory of God in His fullness is at the end.

This is not a sprint, but a marathon: a decathlon: a steeplechase of a race and we simply must endure: remain, persevere,
Be patient!
          Never quit!
                    Never give up!

Along your race you'll be tripped-up, have rocks/darts thrown at you, hit, slapped, spit on, knocked down and you may even fall in a ditch and have to climb out. However, you'll get up and dust yourself off, bandage up your
knees, elbows and head and you'll keep it moving toward the mark for the prize of the high calling of God in Jesus Christ **(Philippians 3:14)**

As you continue to face opposition, distraction, and pitfalls, God in His ever-giving love, grace and mercy has given us the strategy through the word of Jesus Christ how to avoid and guard yourself and fight back the enemy during your race. This is a race that is run to make us strong.

So God may allow the darts, the rocks and ditches, but it's not to take us out, it's to make us stronger. Because strength with endurance makes us **unstoppable!**

The armor of God is a total body protector against what comes at you. **Truth** covers your loins, **Righteousness** covers your breast, the **Gospel of Peace** covers your feet, **Faith** is your shield and depending on how big or how small your faith is, can determine your shields size: large enough to cover your entire body, or small enough to cover a portion at a time. Either way, you have a shield to protect you from the fiery darts of the enemy. There is no need to worry about your back because your brothers and sisters in Christ have your back and because what's behind you is already conquered territory; no enemy back there!

          Advance forward only!
          There is No retreat in God!
      ENDURE until the end & you shall **Overcome!** &
            Be an Overcomer!

<u>*Overcome*</u> in the New Strong's Exhaustive Concordance of the Bible; 3528 in the Greek is **<u>Nikao,</u>** which means to subdue, conquer, prevail, get the victory.

Revelations 2:7 says He that hath ear to hear, let him hear what the Spirit says unto the churches; to him that **overcomes** will I give to eat the tree of life, which is in the midst of the paradise of God.

Revelation 2:11 says He that hath an ear, let him hear what the Spirit says unto the churches; to him that **overcomes**, he shall not be hurt of the second death.

Revelation 2;17 says He that hath an ear, let him hear what the Spirit says unto the churches; to him that overcomes will I give to eat the hidden manna, and will give him a white stone, and in the stone a new name written, which no man knows saving he that receives it.

Revelation 2:26 says And he that overcomes, and keeps my works unto the end, him will I give power over the nations.

Revelation 3:5 says He that overcomes, the same shall be clothed in white raiment and I will not blot out his name out of the book of life, but I will confess his name before my father, and before his angels.

Revelation 3:12 says Him that overcomes will I make a pillar in the temple of my God, and he shall go no more out: and I will write upon him the name of my God, and the name of the city of my God, which is new Jerusalem, which cometh down out of heaven from my God: and I will write upon him my new name.

Revelation 3:21 says To him that overcomes will I grant to sit with me in my throne, even as I also overcame, and am set down with my Father in His throne.

Revelation 21:7 says He that overcomes shall inherit all things; and I will be his God, and he shall be my son.

Jesus overcame this world and Satan. In the wilderness Jesus overcame the temptation of Satan with the word. He would respond to each of Satan's tempt's with **"It is written"** thou shall worship the Lord thy God and Him only shalt thou serve; **It is written**, thou shalt not live by bread alone; **It is written again**, though shalt not tempt the Lord thy God; (**Matthew 4:4-10**).

When He was crucified and died on the cross, He arose from the dead after three days with the keys of hell, death and the grave in His hands. **Revelation 1:18**

> Our acceptance of Jesus and putting our trust in Him
> until the end of our race,
> Guarantees our overcoming!
> Guarantees our victory!
> Guarantees our win!
> Because Jesus has already won! He conquered death and hell!

1 Corinthians 15:57 But thanks be to God, which giveth us the victory through our Lord Jesus Christ.

2 Corinthians 2:14 Now thanks be unto God, which always causeth us to triumph in Christ, and makes manifest the savor of his knowledge by us in every place.

The race is fixed! Mountains have been made low, valleys exalted, crooked places made straight, **Isaiah 40:4**; rough places made plain **Isaiah 45:2**; darkness made light **Isaiah 42:16**; a way made in the wilderness, rivers shall spring forth in the desert, **Isaiah 43:19**; He will show us hidden things. **Isaiah 48:6**; yes even the plans and plots of the enemy He will show us along the way.

2 Corinthians 4:8-9 for we are troubled on every side, yet not distressed, we are perplexed, but not in despair; persecuted, but not forsaken; cast down, but not destroyed.

What doesn't kill us makes us stronger, so the saying goes. And along the way, if we see a brother or a sister who has taken a fall, stagnate or standing still, we should be able to restore such a one in the spirit of meekness; considering thyself lest thou also be tempted."as **Galatians 6:1** says. We have divine appointments with others we are supposed to help, encourage, comfort and strengthen in their journey with Christ.

You must keep going. You must endure! You must overcome! Others are depending on you.

As King Solomon said in **Ecclesiastes 12:13** "…Let us hear the conclusion of the matter;
1. Fear God
2. Keep His commandments, for this is the whole duty of man.

Meaning, this is the bottom line: Run **your race** with **'ENDUREance'; pace yourself** until the end to **overcome**; until Jesus says you're done. Matthew 25:23 **"Well done my good and faithful servant!"**

Father God, I thank You for this race You have given me. I Thank You for Your love, grace and mercy and for the power of the Holy Ghost who helps me in this journey and to run this race. I Thank You for the endurance to go yet another day. I will not be weary in well-doing, but when I feel a little tired; when I begin to slow down; I will rely on Your strength and Your power to get me through. For when I am weak, You show Yourself strong. Thank You! In Jesus name I pray; Amen.

What do you do to encourage yourself to keep going?

I will no longer let my holy name be profaned, and the nations will know that I the Lord am the Holy One in Israel. It is coming! It will surely take place declares the Sovereign Lord. Ezekiel 39:7 NIV

O' Give thanks unto the Lord for He is good: for His mercy endureth forever. Psalm 136:1 KJV

Peace I leave with you, my peace I give unto you; not as the world giveth, give I unto you. Let not your heart be troubled, neither let it be afraid. John 14:27 KJV

When thou saidst, Seek ye my face; my heart said unto thee, Thy face, Lord, will I seek. Psalm 27:8 KJV

He That Dwells

I've read Psalm 91 at least once during my reading of the Bible. After my husband was deployed to Afghanistan in 2011-2012, The Lord directed me to Psalm 91 again. I had recently heard of a story by Peggy Joyce Ruth, her book Psalm 91 tells of the small town of Seadrift, Texas. In this Texas town they posted pictures of their sons, brothers, husbands, nephews who were gone off to war in WWII. One family even had five brothers fighting in this war. The whole town went on a Psalm 91 prayer watch praying this Psalm on a continual basis throughout the war for protection to bring their sons home safely. At the end of the war all of their men returned home. Not a one was lost.

I came upon the Psalm again during my regular reading and felt pressed upon my heart to pray this Psalm everyday for my husband who was away on deployment and I am so glad that I did. Months later after his safe return home, I found out through stories he told about close calls of bombs hitting just on the other side of his bunker, having to drive and shoot their way out of different villages in the desert where negotiations became dangerous, and his driver being guided by The Holy Spirit to safely lead them out of danger. From the stories he told, I know The Holy Spirit protected and guided my husband and those around him from danger. I am so thankful to God.

Pray this Psalm over yourself and your family daily or as often as you are lead. God is faithful. His Word says that He will "hasten His Word to perform it" (Jeremiah 1:12). The Lord God honors His Word prayed back to Him, and He will answer your prayer as well.

Psalms 91:1-16 *(KJV)*

1. He that dwells in the secret place of the most High shall abide under the shadow of the Almighty.
2. I will say of the LORD, He is my refuge and my fortress: my God; in him will I trust.
3. Surely he shall deliver thee from the snare of the fowler, and from the noisome pestilence.
4. He shall cover thee with his feathers, and under his wings shalt thou trust: his truth shall be thy shield and buckler.
5. Thou shalt not be afraid for the terror by night; nor for the arrow that fly by day;
6. Nor for the pestilence that walks in darkness; nor for the destruction that wastes at noonday.
7. A thousand shall fall at thy side, and ten thousand at thy right hand; but it shall not come nigh thee.
8. Only with thine eyes shalt thou behold and see the reward of the wicked.
9. Because thou hast made the LORD, which is my refuge, even the most High, thy habitation;
10. There shall no evil befall thee, neither shall any plague come nigh thy dwelling.
11. For he shall give his angels charge over thee, to keep thee in all thy ways.
12. They shall bear thee up in their hands, lest thou dash thy foot against a stone.
13. Thou shalt tread upon the lion and adder: the young lion and the dragon shalt thou trample under feet.
14. Because he hath set his love upon me, therefore will I deliver him: I will set him on high, because he hath known my name.
15. He shall call upon me, and I will answer him: I will be with him in trouble; I will deliver him, and honor him.
16. With long life will I satisfy Him because he hath remembered my name.

What has God protected you from? What are you thankful for today?

Behold, the fear of the Lord, that is wisdom; and to depart from evil is understanding. Job 28:28 KJV

...I am doing a great work, so that I cannot come down: ...

Nehemiah 6:3 KJV

STRONG

God has given us a strength we don't know we have until we start using it.

The Lord woke me with these words one morning. I wasn't sure of why these words were spoken to my spirit, but I literally heard these words spoken to me as I was waking. I've pondered and thought about these words often since then and I've had to remind myself of these words when attacks from the enemy have come at me or when I've thought about giving up on something because I thought I wasn't strong enough to finish.

**God has given me a strength
I don't know I have,
until I have to use it!**

As a child of God you are Strong because you have the Holy Spirit and the Spirit of Might within you.

You have the DNA of your Creator; your Heavenly Father, Ruler, and Sustainer of the universe and All there is therein. You are:

STRONG!
Mentally STRONG!
Spiritually STRONG!
Emotionally STRONG!
Perseverance STRONG!
Humbly Submitted STRONG!
Covenant Committed STRONG!

Lift up your heads O ye gates; and be ye lifted up ye everlasting doors; and the King of glory shall come in. Who is this King of Glory? The Lord strong and mighty! The Lord mighty in battle. (Psalm 24:7-8)

This doesn't mean that we don't have moments of weakness when we feel like giving up. God is not offended by our weakness. His word says that when we are weak, He is made strong. But what differentiates us is that we keep getting up when we fall down. We keep pushing forward when the enemy butts up against us to try to push us back. No matter how many times we fall or get knocked down or even get knocked out; we get back up and shake it off under the call of the Holy Spirit quietly,

powerfully shouting in our ear from outside the ring; **"Get up! "Get up!" "Keep fighting!"** Keep pressing toward the mark of the high call of God in Jesus Christ. (Phil 3:14)

Have I not commanded thee, be strong and of a good courage; be not afraid, neither be dismayed: for the LORD thy God is with thee whithersoever thou goest. Joshua 1:9

But we have this treasure in earthen vessels, that the excellency of the power may be of God and not of us. We are troubled on every side, yet not distressed; we are perplexed, but not in despair; persecuted, but not forsaken; cast down, but not destroyed. (2 Col 4:7-9)

The bible references at least 365 times to be not afraid, fear not, be strong and courageous; that is once for every day of the year. This is not coincidental! God is intentional and purposeful. We can decree this over our lives each and everyday of the year and be well in line with His word.

Oh no! I don't believe Heaven will be made up of jelly back (as my dear sister in Christ Linda Joy would say), wet noodle, tossed in the towel Christians who laid down when the going got tough or gave up when too much (so they thought), was thrown at them; one thing after another after another. Holy Ghost filled believers have an undeniable power source that won't let them give up, nor turn their backs to God and follow the world again. We have a power that ,when the rubber meets the road, charges us up with even more power to plow and push and keep going to defeat the enemy.

Another movie where the Holy Spirit reminded me of this was in 'Thor Ragnarok'. There is a scene where he first discovers his powers of lightening and electricity. He and the Hulk were in an arena in combat. The Hulk had gotten the upper hand and was pounding on him blow after blow after blow upon Thor's head. And just when you thought there is no way he can take much more of the pounding, he'll die; his eyes began to light up with electricity and lightening and it begins to move throughout his entire body and his arms and pow ya! The hulk is sent a hundred feet into the air and lands with an earthshaking thud to the

ground. Where did this come from? Why had he not used this power before in other movies? He discovered it just when he

needed it the most and had to call upon everything hidden deep within him to not succumb to death.

This is just another one of my movie illustrations where I'll see something in the spirit at a particular moment. Our power is of the Holy Spirit; of the God El Shaddia The Mighty One, not to be taken lightly. But I was reminded in that moment that I always have The Power Source available to me at all times that says, "I can do all things through Christ which strengthens me." (Phil 4:13) And when you need it, as a child of God who has the Holy Spirit residing within you, you can draw upon His power at any time.

God has given us a strength we don't know we have until we start using it. What are your thoughts?

Wisdom is the principal thing, therefore get wisdom: and with all thy getting get understanding. Proverbs 4:7 KJV

Draw nigh to God, and He will draw nigh to you.
James 4:8 KJV

GOD IS

ABSOLUTELY!
Positively

RESOLUTELY!

DEFINITELY!

Most
ASSUREDLY!

Satisfaction
GUARANTEED!

HE IS GOD!!!

Purge Me With Hyssop

One thing I've learned on this journey with Jesus, deliverance is sure-nuff the children's bread of which we will eat and should eat often to keep ourselves clean and pure. We're human, with our human frailties, imperfections and sin we are inherently born into in the image of the fallen Adam. So when we come into the body of Christ as new believers we

bring all of our fears	doubts
wrong teachings	myths
false religion	traditions
perversion	sexual sins
murder	theft
wickedness	coveting
pride	haughtiness

and so much more from which we'll all need deliverance.

Deliverance; to rescue from, the casting out of demons that bring about bondage and bad cycles into our lives. Some of these things begin as early as childhood or maybe occurred as recently as yesterday. Childhood trauma from an accident or death, fears of rejection and abandonment, fear to step out and be seen or heard or to be ourselves who God made us to be, involvement in false teachings, religions and cults, lust and perversion.

As we grow in the knowledge and spirit of Jesus Christ, we'll want to become more like Him and in doing so we have to get rid of those things within us that are not like Christ. We have to seek out the help of an experienced deliverance minister, or ministry that can help us get rid of those non Christ-like characteristics and behaviors.

Submit yourselves therefore to God, resist the devil and he will flee from you. (James 4:7) We have to come out of agreement with the enemy, renounce/denounce them and tell them to GO! Get out! In name of Jesus. Sometimes self-deliverance works okay, but with the more stubborn ones find help from more experienced deliverance ministers.

Once those demons are gone and our houses, our bodies, our spirits are clean, we have to close and lock the doors and windows to keep them out: they will try to come back. The Word says in Matthew 12:43-45

"When the unclean spirit is gone out of a man, he walks through dry places, seeking rest, and findeth none. Then he saith, I will return into my house from whence I came out; and when he is

come, he findeth it empty, swept and garnished. Then goeth he, and taketh with himself seven other spirits more wicked than himself, and they enter in and dwell there: and the last state of the man is worse than the first. Even so shall it be also unto this wicked generation."

We close the doors and lock the windows, but we also must now fill our houses with the Word of God. We cannot leave our houses empty. We have to get the Word in us and be so full of the Word, there will be no room for demons to return. And if and when they try to return, outside of our houses let the warning sign read:
"THIS HOUSE IS PROTECTED BY THE BLOOD OF JESUS"

A scripture that I pray when I feel the need to repent, and ask forgiveness from the Lord is Psalm 51.

1. Have mercy upon me, O God, according to thy lovingkindness: according unto the multitude of thy tender mercies blot out my transgressions.
2 Wash me throughly from mine iniquity, and cleanse me from my sin.
3 For I acknowledge my transgressions: and my sin is ever before me.
4 Against thee, thee only, have I sinned, and done this evil in thy sight: that thou mightest be justified when thou speakest, and be clear when thou judgest.
5 Behold, I was shapen in iniquity; and in sin did my mother conceive me.
6 Behold, thou desirest truth in the inward parts: and in the hidden part thou shalt make me to know wisdom.
7 Purge me with hyssop, and I shall be clean: wash me, and I shall be whiter than snow.
8 Make me to hear joy and gladness; that the bones which thou hast broken may rejoice.
9 Hide thy face from my sins, and blot out all mine iniquities.
10 Create in me a clean heart, O God; and renew a right spirit within me.
11 Cast me not away from thy presence; and take not thy holy spirit from me.
12 Restore unto me the joy of thy salvation; and uphold me with thy free spirit.
13 Then will I teach transgressors thy ways; and sinners shall be converted unto thee.
14 Deliver me from bloodguiltiness, O God, thou God of my salvation: and my tongue shall sing aloud of thy righteousness.
15 O Lord, open thou my lips; and my mouth shall shew forth thy praise.
16 For thou desirest not sacrifice; else would I give it: thou delightest not in burnt offering.
17 The sacrifices of God are a broken spirit: a broken and a contrite heart, O God, thou wilt not despise.
18 Do good in thy good pleasure unto Zion: build thou the walls of Jerusalem.

19 Then shalt thou be pleased with the sacrifices of righteousness, with burnt offering and whole burnt offering: then shall they offer bullocks upon thine altar.

In this Psalm David asks of the Lord:
"wash me thoroughly"
"cleanse me from my sin"
"'purge me with hyssop"
"blot out all mine iniquities"
"deliver me"

I thought about David's words: wash, cleanse, purge, blot. Each of these require at least one of two things: clean water and/or some pressure. I thought of the times I've spilled something on the carpet or on my clothing. What I used to get the spots out were clean water and a little pressure. I'd take a clean cloth and wet it with water, then I'd proceed to put some pressure on the spot to pull up and pull out the stain. Sometimes depending on how bad the stain, I would literally have to apply my whole upper body weight to a stain to blot it out and remove it.
Purge; to get rid of, make clean
Hyssop: a plant used in ancient Hebrew for purification. It has antiseptic properties, it's part of the mint family, and used in expectorants which are used to break up and bring up the phlegm in your chest when congested and now cough up, spit out, get rid of: deliverance.
David prayed for deliverance.
Holy Spirit washes, God the Father applies a little pressure. Purging doesn't feel good. Having pressure applied doesn't feel good, but in the end something is removed and we feel and look better.

Throughout the Word of God it tells us to sanctify ourselves, purify ourselves, set ourselves apart from the world and from what's common; to be peculiar and distinct. When we do this in partnership with the Holy Spirit, we get more and more of the world out of us: we get deliverance.

Seek your Deliverance
Get your Deliverance
Keep your Deliverance

Sanctify yourselves: for tomorrow the Lord will do wonders among you.
Joshua 3:5 KJV

Let everything that hath breath praise the Lord. Praise ye the Lord.
Psalm 150:6 KJV

The Simplicity of the Gospel of Jesus Christ

The Holy Spirit reminded me to ***"Keep it Simple!"***
The Gospel of Jesus Christ doesn't have to be all deep and if one makes it so, they are really trying to draw attention to themselves. Keep the Gospel of Jesus Christ simple:

- **Jesus Christ** Came from heaven, born of a virgin
- **Jesus Christ** Taught with Love of love, to simply believe
- **Jesus Christ** The Kingdom of God is at Hand
- **Jesus Christ** The Perfect Sacrifice
- **Jesus Christ** Sinless; crucified for our sins
- **Jesus Christ** Died and rose again on the 3rd day
- **Jesus Christ** Conquering death, hell and the grave
- **Jesus Christ** You, Me, We, **Freed** by **HIS** shed **Blood**
- **Jesus Christ** Redeemed us unto God the Father
- **Jesus Christ** We'll join HIM again in heaven

Do you believe in Jesus Christ?

Have you accepted Jesus and made Him Lord of your life?

Do you want to ask Him into your heart, and for the Holy Spirit to come in and teach you?

Do it today!
NOW is the time!
Pray this prayer with me:

Dear Jesus, I know that I'm a sinner. I ask that You would forgive me of my sins. I repent Lord. I believe in You Jesus and I ask that You would come into my heart and make me new. I accept the gift of Holy Spirit to help me in my new walk with You. I thank You for Your sacrifice on the cross for me. I now give You my life in return. Help me to love You as I should. In Your name Jesus I pray; Amen.

*Welcome to the kingdom of God!
Now go tell at least three people that you are saved and set free and That you have accepted Jesus Christ as your personal Lord and Savior
Hallelujah!*

How do you feel? Write your testimony here. And be ready at all times to tell your story and tell of the New Hope you have found in Jesus Christ.

_____
_____
_____
_____
_____
_____
_____
_____
_____
_____
_____
_____
_____
_____
_____
_____
_____
_____
_____
_____

If the Son therefore shall make you free, ye shall be free indeed.
John 8:36 KJV

Sanctify yourselves: for tomorrow the Lord will do wonders among you.
Joshua 3:5 KJV

Why?

The Holy Spirit then spoke and said, "Go sit and be still. Get your journal, listen and write.
A question that came to mind was "Why am I feeling lost?" Is this lostness fueled by a need to be wanted, to not feel rejected, to feel important or needed? Or is it fueled by my sincere desire to please God, serve others and work in and for His Kingdom?

It is not by might, nor by power, but by the Spirit of the Lord. We cannot work our way into heaven; it is not of works and our motives, our why must be pure. Yet, I thought,"But how else can I show you Lord that I love you? That I believe in you? How else do I show you?

When you love someone you want to express that love and '**do**' something for them to show them how you feel.
What can I do?
If I have done anything, it doesn't feel like it's enough! I then recognized do I need some deliverance from a spirit of religion, legalism and works? Now granted, we are in a world-wide pandemic and shut down; LOL! And because before the pandemic I hadn't yet found a place to literally put my hands to, although I am a part of the Intercessors prayer group, which I love, I thought I was just sitting around doing nothing it didn't feel like enough! Again, what is this? Why do I feel this way?
But the Lord has built me to work and I do so with gladness of heart, not looking for anything in return. Yet that morning I heard the Spirit of the Lord say, "Get in my presence, get quiet before me, worship, let's have more intimate time alone." Here you can fill that void, strengthen your inner man and get peace in and during this transition. Transition! That is what this is, a transition and place of preparation. This will bring me joy. This will show me that you love me. This is the **'action'** the **'do'** the **'putting your hands to'** that I am looking for right now; getting closer to me says the Lord.
I didn't bring covid19 into existence but I've shut down the world and allowed it to bring things to a halt, so that my people would stop busying themselves with **'things'** to allow them to stop, rest, quiet themselves and really hear from me. I've given them time to get in my presence to get what they need from me. It makes me

happy to hear from my child, to see my child at my table, to have him/her in my presence. The example He gave me was just like you love it when your grown children come home to visit especially when you've not seen them in a while, the joy you feel being able to hug them, see their faces, their smiles, hear their voice up close, touch their hand, feel their skin, run your hands through their hair, all the endearing acts of love to show how much you love them and have missed them, I love that same thing; having you in my presence.

The benefit to you of being in my presence is you are reassured of my love, strengthened in my love, you feel my joy of having you around, you hear my heart and mind for you, the dreams I've instilled in you and the future and hope for you. I will give you counsel on things that may be troubling you. I will give you strategy on how to move forward and give you wisdom when you ask. I will share with you my hearts desire for you and the world you live in. From our communing through the Word and prayer you gain strength, hope, confidence, boldness, faith, recharging, refreshing, newness, refueling: this is my desire. By allowing this world to **'STOP'** It would give you plenty of time to rediscover Me and discover what I truly want for you, my church, the bride of Christ and how to really affect the world and change it, but you need/needed my help. By my Spirit and power and those who took/take the time to ask, seek and knock they will be empowered by my Spirit to do the **true work** of my **love** in my **love** to bring souls into the Kingdom of God, into my presence saving them from the destruction of the 2nd death yet to come for those who reject my son Jesus Christ and His freely given sacrifice and atonement for the sins of the world.

So what can you do for me right now? Sit. Be still. Get before me and hear my voice, know my heart, get nourishment, get strength, get what you need from me, you'll make me happy by doing this. Give me this pleasure, the opportunity to dote upon you with things from heaven; from my Spirit to yours: **THIS IS PLEASING UNTO THE LORD**.

Writing is therapeutic for me. I love it! I'm not a professional writer; not the best at it, but it's what I have done for a very long time as a way to communicate with God, put all of my feelings on

paper and get them out of me, relieve stress, be introspective and keep myself in check. Early in 2020 at the beginning of the COVID19 shut down, I felt the Lord telling me to put this compilation together. A few years earlier He told me to begin telling my story. People needed to start hearing my story as an authentic witness and testimony for Jesus. My question to Him at that time was how do I do this? Where do I do this? Who wants to listen to my story? I don't know anyone. I have very few friends even on Facebook and no influence whatsoever. But I did begin. I began by writing the Prodigal; because that was me: it is my story.

Since hearing His voice telling me to begin telling my story, I've since learned that it doesn't matter the number of Facebook friends you have, or what I think is influence or not, but it makes a difference one-on-one. Those face-to-face conversations at a salon, in a grocery store or waiting in line to vote. These one-on-one conversations matter and this is where my story can make a difference and have an impact. Also, this small compilation of poems, devotions, lessons and what the Lord has spoken to me during our quiet time: me, journaling my journey thus far with Him, can also have an impact and make a difference; one person at a time. One person who may say, I can write a book. One person who may be inspired to pick up the pen again and write songs unto the Lord. One person who may say I feel like drawing again/painting again. One person who may decide to get into Gods presence a little bit more. One person who may pick up the Word of God and begin searching the scriptures for answers instead of looking to man. Once person who may dare to hope again, dream again, trust in God again, not be angry and forgive and choose to live. One person! Just one person at a time! And so, in obedience I wrote and I place this compilation in the hands of the Lord to do with as He pleases, trusting that it gets into the hands of those, one person at a time or many; that He has ordained.

What is the Lord having you do during this world-wide downtime? How have you taken advantage of this time?

___

I AM the Lord thy God…Thou shalt have no other gods before me.

Exodus 20: 1 & 3 KJV

And, behold, I come quickly; and my reward is with me, to give every man according as his work shall be. Revelations 22:12 KJV

But thou shalt remember the Lord thy God, it is He that giveth thee power to make wealth. Deuteronomy 8:18 KJV

Choose you this day whom ye will serve;
Joshua 24:15 KJV

Holy, holy, holy, is the LORD of Hosts: the whole earth is full of His glory.
Isaiah 6:3 KJV

Call unto me, and I will answer thee, and show thee great and mighty things, which thou knows not. Jeremiah 33:3 KJV

Thine ears shall hear a word behind thee, saying this is the way, walk ye in it, when ye turn to the right hand, and when ye turn to the left.
Isaiah 30:21 KJV

Write the vision, make it plain… Habakkuk 2:2 KJV

The Lord thy God in the midst of thee is mighty; He will save, He will rejoice over thee with joy; He will rest in His love, He will joy over thee with singing. Zephaniah 3:17 KJV

The silver is mine, and the gold is mine, saith the Lord of Hosts.
Haggai 2:8 KJV

For I AM the Lord, I change not... Malachi 3:6 KJV

Go into all the world, and preach the gospel to every creature.
Mark 16:15 KJV

Blessed are the pure in heart: for they shall see God.
Matthew 5:8

Walk in the Spirit, and ye shall not fulfill the lust of the flesh.
Galatians 5:16 KJV

May the eyes of your understanding being enlightened; that ye may know what is the hope of His calling, and what the riches of the glory of His inheritance in the saints. Ephesians 1:18 KJV

For God hath not given us the spirit of fear, but of power, and love, and of a sound mind. 2 Timothy 1:7 KJV

Study to show thyself approved unto God, a workman that needeth not to be ashamed, rightly dividing the word of truth.
2 Timothy 2:15 KJV

Blessed is he that readteh and they that hear the words of this prophecy, and keep those things which are written therein: for the time is at hand.
Revelation 1:3 KJV

I AM Alpha and Omega, the beginning and the end, the first and the last.
Revelations 22:13 KJV

Can two walk together, except they be agreed? Amos 3:3 KJV

Call unto me, and I will answer thee, and shew thee great and mighty things, which thou knowest not. Jeremiah 33:3 KJV

...Write the vision, and make it plain upon tables, that he may run that readeth it. Habakkuk 2:2 KJV

And she shall bring forth a son, and thou shalt call His name JESUS:
Matthew 1:21 KJV

...This cup is the new testament in my blood, which is shed for you.
Luke 21:20 KJV

But the fruit of the Spirit is love, joy, peace, longsuffering, gentleness, goodness, faith, meekness, temperance: against such there is no law.
Galatians 5:22-23 KJV

And hath put all things under his feet, and gave him to be the head over all things to the church, Ephesians 1:22 KJV

For me to live is Christ, and to die is gain. Philippians 1:21 KJV

...stir up the gift of God, which is in thee... 2 Timothy 1:6 KJV

But the Lord is faithful, who shall stablish you, and keep you from evil.
2 Thessalonians 3:3 KJV

That being justified by His grace, we should be made heirs according to the hope of eternal life. Titus 3:7 KJV

How shall we escape, if we neglect so great salvation…
Hebrews 2:3 KJV

...work out your own salvation with fear and trembling.
Philippians 2:12 KJV

If we confess our sins, He is faithful and just to forgive us our sins, and cleanse us from all unrighteousness. 1 John 1:9 KJV

Because it is written, Be ye holy; for I AM HOLY. 1 Peter 1:16 KJV

And all thy children shall be taught of the LORD; and great shall be the peace of thy children. Isaiah 54:13 KJV

Be thou exalted, O God, above the heavens: and thy glory above all the earth; Psalm 108:5 KJV

Great is the LORD, and greatly to be praised; and His greatness is unsearchable. Psalm 145:3 KJV

Keep my commandments, and live; and my law as the apple of thine eye. Proverbs 7:2 KJV

...Rise up, my love, my fair one, and come away.
Song of Solomon 2:10 KJV

Surely the Lord GOD will do nothing, but He revealeth His secret unto His servants the prophets. Amos 3:7 KJV

And the LORD spake unto Moses face-to-face, as a man speaketh unto his friend. Exodus 33:11 KJV

...if thy presence go not with me, carry us not up hence.
Exodus 33:15 KJV

...thy people shall be my people, and thy God my God: Ruth 1:16 KJV

Such knowledge is too wonderful for me; it is high, I cannot attain unto it.
Psalm 139:6 KJV

Search me, O God, and know my heart: try me, and know my thoughts:
Psalm 139:23 KJV

Then Jesus declared, "I am the bread of life. Whoever comes to me will never go hungry, and whoever believes in me will never be thirsty.
John 6:35 KJV

Thou wilt shew me the path of life: in thy presence is fulness of joy; at thy right hand there are pleasures for evermore. Psalm 16:11 KJV

For whosoever will save his life shall lose it: but whosoever will lose his life for my sake, the same shall save it. Luke 9:24 KJV

That whosoever believeth in him should not perish, but have eternal life.
John 3:15 KJV

Surely goodness and mercy shall follow me all the days of my life: and I will dwell in the house of the Lord for ever. Psalm 23:6 KJV

Lift up your heads, O ye gates; and be ye lifted up, ye everlasting doors; and the King of glory shall come in. Psalm 24:7 KJV

THE GRACE OF OUR LORD JESUS CHRIST BE WITH YOU ALL.

Amen

Rev 22:21 KJV

www.ingramcontent.com/pod-product-compliance
Lightning Source LLC
Chambersburg PA
CBHW032114090426
42743CB00007B/346